UNLOCK AI FOR BEGINNERS

DISCOVER HOW TO OVERCOME INFORMATION
OVERLOAD WITH SIMPLE INTERACTIVE TECHNIQUES
AND THE LATEST TOOLS & RELIABLE RESOURCES
EVEN IF YOU'RE NOT TECH SAVVY

SYNERGY AI EDITIONS

TABLE OF CONTENTS

Introduction												7

1. FOUNDATIONS OF AI										11
   1.1 What is AI? A Beginner's Introduction					12
   1.2 A Brief History of AI: From Concept to Reality			14
   1.3 Types of AI: Narrow, General, and
   Superintelligent AI										17
   1.4 Everyday AI: How AI is Embedded in Daily Life			19
   1.5 Key Terminologies in AI: A Comprehensive
   Glossary													21
   Interactive Quiz: Foundations of AI						23

2. CORE CONCEPTS AND MECHANISMS							27
   2.1 Machine Learning Basics: An Overview Without
   the Jargon												28
   2.2 Neural Networks Demystified: From Neurons to
   Networks													30
   2.3 Data in AI: The Fuel That Powers Intelligent
   Systems													32
   2.4 Supervised vs. Unsupervised Learning: What's
   the Difference?											34
   2.5 Reinforcement Learning: How Machines Learn
   from Rewards												36
   Interactive Quiz: Core Concepts and Mechanisms			39

3. TOOLS AND TECHNOLOGIES									43
   3.1 AI-Powered Apps: Everyday Tools for Beginners		46
   3.2 Visual Programming with AI: Tools and
   Techniques												48
   3.3 AI in the Cloud: Leveraging Cloud-Based AI
   Services													50
   3.4 Open-Source AI: Exploring Free and Powerful
   Resources												52

4. PRACTICAL APPLICATIO   57
   4.1 AI in Healthcare: Revolutionizing Diagnosis and
   Treatment   58
   4.2 AI in Finance: Enhancing Security and Predictive
   Analytics   60
   4.3 AI in Retail: Personalizing Shopping Experiences   63
   4.4 AI in Transportation: The Road to Autonomous
   Vehicles   65
   4.5 AI in Creative Fields: Generating Art, Music, and
   Writing   68

5. HANDS-ON PROJECTS   75
   5.1 Building Your First AI Model: A Step-by-Step
   Guide   76
   5.2 Creating a Chatbot: Practical Exercise for
   Beginners   78
   5.3 Sentiment Analysis with AI: Understanding
   Social Media   81
   5.4 Image Recognition: Developing a Simple AI
   Vision System   83
   5.5 AI in Personal Projects: Bringing Ideas to Life   85

6. ETHICAL AND SOCIETAL IMPLICATION   91
   6.1 Privacy Concerns: Safeguarding Personal Data in
   AI Systems   94
   6.2 AI and Job Displacement: Preparing for the
   Future of Work   97
   6.3 Bias in AI: Identifying and Mitigating Risks   100
   6.4 AI Governance: Policies and Regulations Around
   the World   102

7. FUTURE TRENDS IN AI   109
   7.1 Quantum Computing and AI: A Revolutionary
   Combination   110
   7.2 AI in Space Exploration: Beyond Earthly
   Applications   112
   7.3 The Evolution of AI: Future Technologies and
   Innovations   114
   7.4 AI and Human Interaction: The Next Frontier   117
   7.5 Predicting AI Trends: What's Next in the AI
   World?   119

8. CAREER PROSPECTS IN AI 125
8.1 AI in the Job Market: Skills in Demand 126
8.2 Transitioning Careers: How to Pivot into AI
Roles 129
8.3 AI Certifications: Boosting Your Resume 131
8.4 Networking in the AI Community: Building
Connections 133
8.5 Crafting a Career Plan: Steps to Achieve Your AI
Goals 136

9. RESOURCES FOR CONTINUOUS LEARNING 141
9.1 AI Books and Publications: Must-Reads for
Enthusiasts 144
9.2 AI Conferences and Workshops: Engaging with
the Community 147
9.3 Podcasts and Webinars: Listening to AI Experts 149
9.4 Curated Resource Lists: Tools and Websites for
Deep Dives 151

10. SPECIAL TOPICS IN AI 157
10.1 Natural Language Processing (NLP): AI's
Understanding of Human Language 158
10.2 Generative AI: Creating New Content with AI 161
10.3 AI in Ethics and Philosophy: Debating AI's Role
in Society 165

Conclusion 173
Quiz answers 177
References 179
About the Author 183

INTRODUCTION

It's a chilly morning in December, and you're huddled over a cup of coffee, scrolling through your phone. Your virtual assistant chimes in with a reminder for your meeting, while a recommendation for your next binge-watch, pops up on your streaming service. The weather app suggests you grab an umbrella before heading out, and your fitness tracker nudges you to take a few more steps. These everyday conveniences are powered by Artificial Intelligence (AI), faintly weaving itself into the fabric of our daily routines. We have all been using it and don't think about it.

AI is no longer the stuff of science fiction; it's here, it's now, and it's everywhere. From the voice that guides you through traffic to the algorithms that curate your social media feed, AI is transforming how we live, work, and play. Yet, for many, the idea of understanding AI feels daunting. The jargon, the complexity, and the sheer volume of information can be overwhelming.

But here's the exciting part – understanding AI doesn't have to be intimidating. In fact, it can be fun, engaging, and immensely rewarding. That's where this book comes in. "Unlocking AI: A Beginner's Journey" is crafted to demystify AI for you, making it accessible and enjoyable, regardless of your technical background.

Consider this your personal guidebook to the world of AI. We'll journey together through step-by-step instructions, interactive exercises, and up-to-date resources. Think of it as a conversation with a knowledgeable friend who's here to help you navigate the landscape of AI, one easy-to-understand concept at a time. Let's go on this fun and exciting journey together.

Our goal is simple: to make AI accessible to everyone, whether you're a recent graduate, a retiree, or anywhere in between. We understand that the prospect of diving into AI can be intimidating. Maybe you're worried about the coding aspect or feel over-whelmed by the sheer amount of information out there. We've designed this book to address those concerns and break down the barriers to entry.

Each chapter of this book will build your confidence incremen-tally. We'll start with foundational concepts, move through prac-tical applications, and end with hands-on projects that solidify your understanding. Real-world examples and interactive exer-cises will punctuate our journey, ensuring that you not only learn but also get to apply what you've learned in meaningful ways.

Every chapter concludes with additional resources for further exploration. These include online tools, exercises, and updates to keep your knowledge fresh and relevant. Trust us, by the end of this book, you'll feel empowered and sure of your ability to under-stand and use AI.

Synergy AI Editions, your guide on this journey, has a history of making complex topics accessible. Our previous publication, "Understanding Generative AI for Business Leaders," received accolades for its practical and easy-to-understand strategies. We are committed to continuing this tradition, providing actionable insights you can apply immediately.

We invite you to engage actively with the content of this book. Use the online resources and tools provided, share your progress and insights with the AI learning community, and most importantly, enjoy the journey. AI has the potential to transform lives in unimaginable ways, and understanding it is the first step in harnessing its power.

So, whether you're 18 or 99, a tech enthusiast, or someone who has never touched a line of code, this book is for you. We'll address common concerns and bust myths and answer the questions you've been too afraid to ask. By the time you finish, you'll understand AI and have the confidence to explore it further.

Let's start this journey together. Welcome to "Unlock AI for Beginners" Prepare to unlock the potential of AI in a way that's accessible, practical, and above all, fun.

1

FOUNDATIONS OF AI

Y ou're cruising down the highway in your car, and without you even noticing, your vehicle adjusts its speed to match the flow of traffic. Your GPS suggests an alternate route to avoid congestion, and your favorite playlist starts automatically. These seamless interactions are made possible by Artificial Intelligence (AI), quietly working behind the scenes to make your life easier. AI has come a long way from being a concept in sci-fi movies to an integral part of our daily lives. Whether it's streaming recommendations, voice-activated assistants, or smart home devices, AI is here to stay.

AI is not just a buzzword; it's a transformative technology that touches almost every aspect of our lives. From healthcare diagnostics to personalized shopping experiences, AI is ever-present. Yet, despite its prevalence, the concept of AI can still seem intimidating. Many of us find ourselves asking, "What exactly is AI?" This chapter aims to demystify AI, breaking it down into digestible, relatable terms. We'll explore its foundational concepts and highlight its importance in modern society. You don't need a technical background to understand this—just a curiosity about how things work.

1.1 WHAT IS AI? A BEGINNER'S INTRODUCTION

Artificial Intelligence, or AI, is the simulation of human intelligence in machines. In simpler terms, AI enables machines to mimic cognitive functions such as learning, problem-solving, and decision-making. Think of AI as the brain behind various technologies that perform tasks usually requiring human intelligence. For instance, when your smartphone predicts the next word in your text message or when a virtual assistant schedules your appointments, that's AI at work. It's like having an intelligent helper that can process information, learn from it, and make decisions based on that learning.

Unlike traditional programming that follows pre-defined rules, AI systems learn from data and improve over time. Traditional software executes specific instructions given by a programmer. AI, on the other hand, adapts and evolves by analyzing patterns in data. For example, a spam email filter doesn't just follow a set of rules. It learns from thousands of emails, identifying patterns that distinguish spam from legitimate messages. Over time, it becomes more accurate, adapting to new types of spam as they emerge. This ability to learn and adapt is what sets AI apart from conventional programming.

The importance of AI in modern life cannot be talked about enough. AI-powered virtual assistants like Siri and Alexa make our lives more convenient by handling tasks such as setting reminders and answering queries. Recommendation systems on platforms like Netflix and Amazon personalize our user experience by suggesting content based on our preferences. Although autonomous vehicles are still in development, promise to revolutionize transportation by reducing accidents and improving traffic flow. AI is also making strides in healthcare, where algorithms analyze medical images to assist in diagnosing diseases and personalized treatment plans that are crafted using AI insights. The applications are vast and growing every day.

Let's introduce some key areas within AI to give you a roadmap of what's to come. One major field is Machine Learning (ML), which involves algorithms that learn from data to make predictions or decisions. For instance, a machine learning algorithm can predict stock market trends based on historical data. Another crucial area is Natural Language Processing (NLP), where AI systems understand and generate human language. This is what powers chatbots and language translation services. Then, we have Computer Vision (CV), which enables machines to interpret and make decisions based on visual data. This technology is used in facial recognition systems and autonomous vehicles. These are just a few of the many fields within AI that we'll explore in this book.

Each of these areas has its own set of challenges and opportunities, and understanding them will give you a comprehensive view of AI's potential. We'll dive deeper into these topics in the following chapters, providing you with step-by-step instructions, interactive exercises, and real-world examples. Our aim is to make AI accessible to everyone, regardless of your technical background. By the end of this book, you'll understand AI and feel confident in your ability to use it in your own life.

So, whether you're a student, a professional, or someone simply curious about AI, this book is for you. We'll tackle common concerns, answer your questions, and provide you with the tools you need to navigate the world of AI. From practical applications to ethical considerations, our journey through AI will be thorough and engaging. Get ready to unlock the potential of AI and discover how it can enrich your life in ways you never imagined.

1.2 A BRIEF HISTORY OF AI: FROM CONCEPT TO REALITY

Imagine it's the early 1950s, and a brilliant mathematician named Alan Turing is pondering an intriguing question: Can machines think? This question led him to write his seminal paper, "Computing Machinery and Intelligence," where he introduced the Turing Test. The Turing Test aimed to determine a machine's ability to exhibit intelligent behavior indistinguishable from that of a human. This was one of the earliest theoretical foundations of AI, setting the stage for decades of research and development. Turing's work was pivotal, sparking curiosity and laying down the fundamental challenge that AI researchers would strive to meet.

Fast forward to 1956, when a group of researchers gathered at Dartmouth College for a summer workshop. This event, known as the Dartmouth Conference, is often considered the birth of AI as a formal field of study. The attendees, including pioneers like John McCarthy and Marvin Minsky, envisioned creating machines that could simulate human intelligence. They coined the term "Artificial Intelligence" and set ambitious goals for the nascent field. Although progress was slower than anticipated, this conference marked a significant milestone, establishing AI as a legitimate area of scientific inquiry.

In the following years, AI research saw several key breakthroughs. One notable example is ELIZA, a program developed in 1966 by Joseph Weizenbaum at MIT. ELIZA mimicked a psychotherapist, engaging users in conversations by recognizing key words and responding with pre-programmed scripts. While ELIZA's understanding was superficial, it demonstrated the potential of natural language processing and paved the way for more sophisticated conversational agents. By the 1980s, expert systems emerged, which were designed to mimic the decision-making abilities of human experts. These systems, such as MYCIN for medical diagnosis, used rule-based approaches to solve specific problems, showcasing AI's practical applications.

However, the path to AI's current prominence wasn't smooth. The field experienced periods of reduced funding and interest, known as AI winters. The first AI winter occurred in the 1970s when initial optimism declined due to the slow progress and limitations of early AI systems. Funding dried up, and many researchers shifted their focus to other areas. Another AI winter struck in the late 1980s and early 1990s as the limitations of rule-based systems became apparent. This period of stagnation was marked by skepticism about AI's feasibility and potential.

Yet, AI experienced resurgences fueled by technological advancements. The 1990s saw a renewed interest in AI, driven by increases in computing power and the availability of large datasets.

Researchers began exploring new approaches, such as Machine Learning (ML), which allowed systems to learn from data rather than relying solely on pre-defined rules. This shift marked a significant turning point, laying the groundwork for modern AI.

In recent years, we've witnessed remarkable advancements in AI, particularly with the advent of Deep Learning (DL). In 2012, a groundbreaking moment occurred when AlexNet, a deep learning model, won the ImageNet competition by a significant margin. Developed by Alex Krizhevsky, Ilya Sutskever, and Geoffrey Hinton, AlexNet demonstrated the power of Convolutional Neural Networks (CNNs) for image recognition. This success spurred a wave of innovation, leading to rapid progress in various AI applications.

One of the most notable achievements in AI came in 2016 when AlphaGo, developed by DeepMind, defeated the world champion Go player Lee Sedol. Go is an ancient board game with an immense number of possible moves, making it a formidable challenge for AI. AlphaGo's victory showcased the potential of reinforcement learning and neural networks, capturing the world's attention and highlighting AI's capabilities.

As we move forward, AI continues to evolve, with new developments and applications emerging regularly. From self-driving cars to advanced natural language processing systems, the possibilities seem endless. The history of AI is a testament to human ingenuity and perseverance, illustrating how far we've come and hinting at the exciting future that lies ahead.

1.3 TYPES OF AI: NARROW, GENERAL, AND SUPERINTELLIGENT AI

Imagine you're sitting at home, speaking to your virtual assistant, asking it to play your favorite music or set a reminder for tomorrow's meeting. This is a prime example of Narrow AI, also known as Weak AI. Narrow AI is designed to perform specific tasks efficiently, but it lacks general cognitive abilities. It's like a master of one trade rather than a jack of all. Voice assistants like Siri and recommendation algorithms on streaming services fall into this category. They excel at their designated tasks, such as understanding voice commands or suggesting movies based on your viewing history, but they don't possess broader intelligence beyond these functions. Chatbots in customer service are another illustration; they can answer frequently asked questions and handle basic inquiries but cannot engage in deep, meaningful conversations on various topics.

Now, let's turn our attention to General AI, often referred to as Strong AI. This concept remains largely theoretical and represents the idea of machines possessing the ability to perform any intellectual task that a human can do. Imagine a machine that understands natural language and writes a novel, solves complex equations, and debates philosophical questions—all with human-like proficiency. General AI would have the cognitive flexibility to learn and adapt across a wide range of tasks, much like a human being. However, despite significant advancements in AI, achieving General AI is still a distant goal. Current technologies haven't reached this level of sophistication, and much of the research in this area remains speculative, driven by hope and caution.

The idea of Superintelligent AI takes the concept even further. Superintelligent AI would surpass human intelligence in all aspects, from creativity to problem-solving and emotional intelligence. This type of AI could potentially solve problems beyond human comprehension, making strides in fields like medicine, climate science, and beyond. However, the prospect of Superintelligent AI raises significant ethical and societal questions. If a machine becomes more intelligent than its creators, who controls it? How do we ensure it aligns with human values and interests? The potential for such AI to operate independently or even develop goals counter to human well-being is a subject of intense debate and concern among experts.

Comparing these three types of AI highlights the current state of technology and future aspirations. Presently, all AI systems in use are examples of Narrow AI. They are specialized, efficient, and continuously improving but confined to specific tasks. General AI, with its broader, human-like capabilities, remains a theoretical goal that researchers are striving to achieve. Superintelligent AI, while captivating the imagination, is fraught with uncertainties and ethical dilemmas. The journey from Narrow to General to Superintelligent AI involves not just technical advancements but also careful consideration of the implications for society.

In our daily lives, we interact with Narrow AI, benefiting from its specialized skills. From the convenience of voice assistants to the personalized touch of recommendation systems, Narrow AI enhances our experiences in countless ways. However, understanding the distinctions between these types of AI helps us appreciate the current capabilities and limitations of the technology. It also prepares us for the ongoing discussions about the future of AI, its potential, and the ethical considerations it brings to the forefront. As we explore these themes further, keep in mind the transformative power of AI and the responsibilities that come with harnessing it.

1.4 EVERYDAY AI: HOW AI IS EMBEDDED IN DAILY LIFE

Imagine waking up to your smartphone's gentle alarm, which adjusts based on your sleep patterns. As you unlock your phone with facial recognition, it greets you with a weather update and your daily schedule. This seamless experience is powered by AI, which has become an integral part of our personal devices. Your smartphone uses AI for predictive text, suggesting the next word in your message, and for voice recognition, enabling hands-free commands. Smart home devices, like thermostats, learn your preferences and adjust the temperature accordingly, while security systems use AI to distinguish between familiar faces and potential intruders. Wearables, such as fitness trackers, monitor your health metrics, providing insights into your physical activity and sleep quality. These AI-powered devices enhance our daily routines, making life more convenient and personalized.

AI has also revolutionized online services, improving how we interact with digital platforms. Search engines like Google use complex algorithms to deliver the most relevant results based on your queries. Social media platforms employ AI to curate content, showing posts and updates tailored to your interests. This personalization extends to streaming services, where recommendation systems suggest movies, music, and shows you might enjoy based on your viewing history. AI ensures that your online experiences are not only efficient but also engaging. By analyzing vast amounts of data, AI helps these services understand user behavior, optimize content delivery, and enhance overall user satisfaction.

In the realm of transportation, AI is driving significant advancements, from autonomous vehicles to ride-sharing apps. Companies like Tesla are at the forefront of developing self-driving cars, which rely on AI to navigate roads, recognize obstacles, and make real-time decisions. These vehicles promise to reduce accidents and improve traffic flow, making transportation safer and more efficient. Ride-sharing platforms like Uber and Lyft use AI to optimize routes, predict demand, and match riders with drivers. AI also plays a crucial role in traffic management systems, where smart traffic lights adjust their timing based on real-time traffic conditions, reducing congestion and travel time. These innovations are transforming how we move from place to place, making transportation smarter and more responsive.

Healthcare is another sector where AI is making a profound impact. AI algorithms analyze medical images with remarkable accuracy, assisting doctors in diagnosing conditions such as cancer and heart disease. These systems can detect abnormalities that might be missed by the human eye, improving early detection and treatment outcomes. Personalized treatment plans are crafted using AI, which can analyze a patient's medical history, genetic information, and lifestyle factors to recommend tailored therapies. Virtual health assistants powered by AI provide patients with instant access to medical advice, appointment scheduling, and health monitoring. These assistants can answer queries, remind patients to take their medication, and even alert healthcare providers in case of emergencies. AI is enhancing patient care, making diagnostics more accurate, and streamlining administrative tasks in healthcare settings.

In each of these areas, AI is not just a technological marvel but a practical tool that improves our daily lives. It learns from our behaviors, adapts to our needs, and makes decisions that enhance our experiences. By understanding how AI is embedded in everyday life, we can appreciate its convenience and efficiency and feel more confident in exploring its potential further. Whether it's through personal devices, online services, transportation, or healthcare, AI is here to stay, continually evolving to meet the challenges and opportunities of the modern world.

1.5 KEY TERMINOLOGIES IN AI: A COMPREHENSIVE GLOSSARY

When stepping into the realm of AI, understanding its key terms is crucial. Let's begin with some essential AI terms you'll encounter throughout this book. An algorithm is a set of rules or instructions designed to solve a problem or perform a task. Think of it as a recipe in a cookbook—each step needs to be followed to achieve the desired outcome. A neural network is a computational model inspired by the human brain's structure. It consists of interconnected nodes or "neurons" that process data in layers, mimicking how the brain works to recognize patterns and make decisions.

In the context of machine learning, several terms are frequently used. Training data refers to the dataset used to teach an AI model. It's the information fed into the model for it to learn and make predictions. Imagine trying to learn a new language; the training data would be your vocabulary lists and grammar rules. Overfitting occurs when a model learns the training data too well, capturing noise and details that don't generalize to new data. It's like memorizing practice test questions without understanding the underlying concepts, leading to poor performance on actual exams.

Understanding AI in practice involves familiarizing yourself with specific applications. Natural Language Processing (NLP) is AI's ability to understand and generate human language. This technology powers chatbots, language translation services, and text analysis tools. Computer Vision enables machines to interpret visual information from the world, such as recognizing objects in images or videos. These applications are crucial in fields like surveillance, healthcare, and autonomous driving, where visual data needs to be analyzed quickly and accurately.

Ethical and societal implications of AI are also essential to grasp. AI Ethics refers to the study of moral issues surrounding AI development and use. It addresses questions about fairness, accountability, and transparency in AI systems. For example, an AI that decides who gets a loan must be fair and unbiased. Bias in AI is a systematic error that leads to unfair outcomes, often rooted in biased training data. If an AI system is trained on data that reflects societal prejudices, it can perpetuate those biases, leading to discriminatory decisions.

Let's consider a practical scenario to make these terms even more approachable. Imagine you're using a streaming service. The recommendation system suggests movies based on your viewing history. Here, the algorithm processes your past behavior (training data) to predict what you'll enjoy next. If the recommendations are too narrow, focusing only on one genre, the system might be overfitting to your data. NLP is at work when you use voice commands to search for a movie, and computer vision helps in tagging and categorizing video content automatically. The streaming service must ensure its algorithms are fair, avoiding bias in suggestions and providing diverse content to all users.

Understanding these key terms will equip you with the vocabulary needed to navigate AI discussions confidently. As you progress through this book, these terms will become second nature, allowing you to grasp more complex concepts and applications. Each chapter will build on this foundation, introducing new terms and reinforcing your understanding with interactive exercises and real-world examples.

In this exploration of AI, we aim to make complex ideas simple and relatable. Our goal is not just to inform but to empower you.

By breaking down technical jargon and presenting it in an accessible way, we hope to build your confidence in understanding and discussing AI. This book is designed to be your companion, guiding you through the fascinating world of AI with clarity and ease.

As we conclude this section, remember that AI is not just a technological advancement but a tool that has the potential to transform lives. By learning its language, you open the door to endless possibilities. Embrace the journey ahead with curiosity and enthusiasm, knowing that each step brings you closer to mastering the fundamentals of AI.

INTERACTIVE QUIZ: FOUNDATIONS OF AI

1. Introduction to AI

- **Question**: What is Artificial Intelligence (AI)?

  a) A simulation of human intelligence in machines
  b) A form of manual programming where rules are pre-defined
  c) A type of hardware used in computers

- **Question**: How does AI differ from traditional programming?

  a) AI systems learn and adapt from data, while traditional programming follows pre-defined rules
  b) AI is less efficient than traditional programming
  c) AI requires no data to function

2. History of AI

- **Question**: Who is credited with laying the early theoretical foundations of AI through the Turing Test?

  a) Marvin Minsky
  b) Alan Turing
  c) John McCarthy

- **Question**: What was the significance of the Dartmouth Conference in 1956?

  a) It was the first time AI was used in a commercial product
  b) The term "Artificial Intelligence" was coined, and AI became a formal field of study
  c) It marked the first AI winter

3. Types of AI

- **Question**: Which type of AI is exemplified by virtual assistants like Siri and Alexa?

  a) General AI
  b) Superintelligent AI
  c) Narrow AI

- **Question**: What is the primary concern associated with Superintelligent AI?

  a) It may not be able to perform tasks as efficiently as humans
  b) It could surpass human intelligence, leading to ethical and control issues

c) It cannot learn from data

4. AI in Daily Life

- **Question**: Which of the following is an example of AI embedded in everyday life?

a) A microwave oven
b) A smartphone that uses facial recognition to unlock
c) A manual typewriter

- **Question**: How does AI improve transportation systems?

a) By creating better roads
b) Through autonomous vehicles and ride-sharing platforms optimizing routes and traffic
c) By controlling traffic lights without data

5. Key Terminologies in AI

- **Question**: What is an algorithm in the context of AI?

a) A hardware component in a computer
b) A set of rules or instructions designed to solve a problem
c) A random process that generates data

- **Question**: What is overfitting in machine learning?

a) When a model learns the training data too well, capturing noise that doesn't generalize to new data
b) When a model fails to learn from the training data
c) When a model performs well on all data without errors

2

CORE CONCEPTS AND
MECHANISMS

P icture this: You're on your favorite streaming platform, and it seems to know exactly what you want to watch next. How does it do that? The answer lies in a fascinating technology known as machine learning. As you navigate through recommendations, personalized playlists, and smart search results, you're interacting with systems that have been trained to understand your preferences and predict your choices. Machine learning works quietly behind the scenes, making your digital experiences seamless and intuitive. But what exactly is machine learning, and how does it manage these feats?

2.1 MACHINE LEARNING BASICS: AN OVERVIEW WITHOUT THE JARGON

Machine learning is a type of artificial intelligence that enables computers to learn from data and improve their performance on tasks without being explicitly programmed. Imagine teaching a child to recognize different animals. Instead of giving the child a static list of rules to follow, you show them pictures of various animals and provide their names. Over time, the child learns to identify and categorize animals based on the features they've observed. Similarly, machine learning algorithms learn patterns from data and use those patterns to make predictions or decisions.

There are different types of machine learning, each with its unique approach to learning from data. **Supervised learning** is like having a teacher guide you through every step. In this method, the algorithm is trained using labeled data, where each example is paired with the correct output. For instance, to teach an AI to recognize cats and dogs, you'd provide a dataset with images labeled as 'cat' or 'dog.' The algorithm learns to map input (images) to the correct output (labels) by finding patterns in the training data. Once trained, it can predict labels for new, unseen images.

Unsupervised learning, on the other hand, operates without labeled data. Imagine trying to sort a box of mixed candies without knowing their types. You'd group them based on similarities in color, shape, or taste. In unsupervised learning, the algorithm identifies hidden patterns or structures within the data. Clustering is a common unsupervised learning technique where the algorithm groups similar data points together. For example, it can segment customers into different groups based on purchasing behavior, allowing businesses to target specific customer segments more effectively.

Reinforcement learning is akin to learning through trial and error. Picture a dog learning to fetch a ball. It tries different actions, like running in various directions, and receives rewards (praise or treats) for the right actions. The dog learns to maximize rewards by repeating successful behaviors. In reinforcement learning, an agent interacts with an environment, takes actions, and receives feedback in the form of rewards or penalties. Over time, the agent learns to take actions that maximize cumulative rewards. This approach is used in training autonomous vehicles and game-playing AI, where the system learns strategies through repeated interactions with the environment.

Key components of machine learning models include **features, labels**, and **algorithms**. Features are individual measurable properties or characteristics of the data. For instance, in a dataset of houses, features might include the number of bedrooms, square footage, and location. Labels are the output or target variables that the model aims to predict, such as the price of the house. Algorithms are the mathematical procedures used to model the data and make predictions. Just as a chef uses different recipes to create various dishes, data scientists select algorithms that best suit the problem at hand.

Machine learning applications are diverse and impactful. Consider spam email detection, where algorithms analyze email content to classify messages as spam or not spam, protecting your inbox from unwanted emails. In manufacturing, predictive maintenance uses machine learning to analyze data from machinery sensors, predicting failures before they occur and minimizing downtime. Personalized marketing leverages machine learning to analyze consumer behavior, delivering targeted ads that resonate with individual preferences, thereby increasing engagement and sales.

Machine learning's ability to learn from data and improve over time makes it a powerful tool in various fields. Understanding these core concepts will better equip you to appreciate the technology that shapes our digital world.

2.2 NEURAL NETWORKS DEMYSTIFIED: FROM NEURONS TO NETWORKS

Imagine you're looking at a photograph, and within seconds, your brain identifies a smiling face, a sunny sky, and a bustling street. This rapid recognition is thanks to your brain's intricate network of neurons, which constantly process and transmit information. Neural networks in artificial intelligence are inspired by this biological marvel. Just as neurons in your brain send signals to each other, AI's neural networks mimic this process to recognize patterns and make decisions. Think of it as creating a digital brain that can learn from experience and improve over time.

At the heart of neural networks are neurons, the individual processing units that handle bits of information. These digital neurons are organized into layers. The input layer receives external data, much like your senses receive signals from the environment. Hidden layers, which can be several, process this data through complex computations, akin to how different regions of the brain analyze sensory input. Finally, the output layer delivers the result, whether it's identifying an object in a photo or predicting the next word in a sentence. Connections between neurons, known as synapses in the brain, play a crucial role in transmitting these signals, with each connection assigned a weight that determines its importance.

Learning in neural networks involves adjusting these weights to improve performance, a process guided by methods like **backpropagation** and **gradient descent**. Backpropagation is a technique used to fine-tune the weights by calculating the error in the output and distributing this error back through the network. Think of it as receiving feedback from a teacher and using it to correct your mistakes. Gradient descent is an optimization algorithm that helps minimize this error by iteratively adjusting the weights in small steps. Imagine climbing down a hill to find the lowest point; gradient descent guides each step to ensure you reach the bottom efficiently.

There are various types of neural networks, each designed for specific tasks. **Feedforward** neural networks are the simplest, with data flowing in one direction from input to output. They're like a one-way street where information moves straightforwardly through the layers. **Convolutional** neural networks (CNNs) are specialized for image recognition tasks. They use convolutional layers to detect features like edges and textures, making them adept at identifying objects in photos. Picture a CNN as an artist who first sketches the outlines before adding details. **Recurrent** neural networks (RNNs) excel in handling sequential data like text and time series. They have connections that loop back, allowing them to retain information from previous steps. It's similar to how you remember the context of a story as you read each page.

These neural networks are behind many of the intelligent systems we interact with daily. When your smartphone recognizes your face to unlock, it's likely using a CNN. When you type a message, and your phone predicts the next word, an RNN is at work. These networks also power more complex applications, like translating languages in real-time or generating realistic images from scratch. Understanding how these networks function demystifies the technology and opens up a world of possibilities for innovation and creativity.

2.3 DATA IN AI: THE FUEL THAT POWERS INTELLIGENT SYSTEMS

Imagine you're baking a cake. The ingredients you use—flour, eggs, sugar to determine the final taste and texture. In the world of AI, data is like those ingredients. It's the critical component that drives the learning and decision-making processes of AI systems. Without data, AI systems would be like chefs with empty pantries, unable to create anything meaningful. Data provides the information AI systems need to identify patterns and make predictions, much like how recipes guide a chef.

There are various types of data used in AI, each with its unique characteristics and uses. Structured data is organized in a clear and easily searchable format, often stored in databases. Think of it as an Excel spreadsheet with rows and columns. Each column represents a feature, such as age, income, or purchase history, and each row is a data point. This type of data is easy to manipulate and analyze, making it ideal for tasks like customer segmentation or fraud detection.

On the other hand, unstructured data is more free-form and doesn't fit neatly into tables. Examples include text documents, social media posts, and images. Imagine a box filled with random photos and handwritten notes—each item holds valuable information, but it's not organized in any specific way. AI systems need to work harder to extract meaningful insights from unstructured data, often using advanced techniques like natural language processing for text analysis or computer vision for image recognition.

Semi-structured data falls somewhere in between. It contains elements of both structured and unstructured data. JSON and XML files are classic examples where the data is organized in a hierarchical format but doesn't fit neatly into rows and columns. Think of it as a recipe book where some instructions are listed step-by-step, while others are written as paragraphs. AI systems can navigate this complexity to extract useful information, making semi-structured data versatile for various applications.

Collecting and preparing data for AI models involves several crucial steps. Data collection is the first stage, where relevant data is gathered from various sources. This could be anything from customer transaction records to sensor readings from industrial equipment. Next, data cleaning ensures that the collected data is free of errors and inconsistencies. Imagine sorting through your pantry and discarding expired ingredients. Similarly, data normalization scales the data to a standard range, ensuring that different features are comparable. It's like measuring all your ingredients in the same unit—cups, grams, or ounces—so the recipe turns out just right.

However, working with data in AI has its challenges. Data quality is a significant concern. Ensuring that data is accurate, complete, and reliable is crucial for building effective AI models. Poor quality data is like using spoiled ingredients in a recipe, leading to undesirable results. Data quantity is another critical factor. Having sufficient data to train models effectively is essential. Imagine trying to learn a new language with only a handful of vocabulary words; it's unlikely you'll become fluent. Similarly, small datasets limit the AI model's ability to learn and generalize.

Data privacy is an increasingly important issue. Protecting sensitive information while using it to train AI models is a delicate balance. Think of it as sharing a family recipe—you want to keep certain elements secret while still allowing others to enjoy the dish. Ensuring data privacy involves techniques like data anonymization and encryption to safeguard personal information.

Navigating these challenges is vital for leveraging data effectively in AI. Understanding data's role in AI, the types of data used, and the process of preparing data helps you appreciate the complexity and importance of this foundational element. Data is the fuel that powers intelligent systems, enabling them to learn, adapt, and make informed decisions.

2.4 SUPERVISED VS. UNSUPERVISED LEARNING: WHAT'S THE DIFFERENCE?

Imagine you're teaching a child to recognize different fruits. You show them pictures of apples, oranges, and bananas, each labeled with its name. This approach mirrors supervised learning in AI, where algorithms learn from labeled data. In this method, you provide the AI with a dataset that includes inputs (like images) and their corresponding outputs (labels). During the training phase, the AI model analyzes these examples, identifying patterns and relationships between the inputs and labels. For instance, it learns that apples are usually red or green and round, while bananas are yellow and elongated. Once trained, the model enters the prediction phase, where it can accurately identify new, unlabeled images of fruits based on the patterns it learned.

Now, consider a different scenario where you hand the child a basket of mixed fruits without any labels. You ask them to sort the fruits into groups based on similarities. This method resembles unsupervised learning, where the AI is given data without labels and tasked with finding patterns or structures within it. In this process, the AI explores the data, grouping similar items together through clustering. For example, it might group red, round fruits together and long, yellow fruits in another cluster. Another technique used in unsupervised learning is dimensionality reduction, which simplifies the data by reducing the number of variables while preserving its essential characteristics. This helps in visualizing complex datasets and uncovering hidden patterns.

The key differences between supervised and unsupervised learning lie in their approaches and applications. Supervised learning is highly effective for tasks such as classification and regression, where the goal is to predict a specific outcome based on input data. For example, email spam detection uses supervised learning to classify emails as spam or not spam based on labeled examples. Medical diagnosis is another application where algorithms analyze patient data and predict the likelihood of diseases. Supervised learning excels in scenarios where accurate predictions are crucial and labeled data is readily available.

In contrast, unsupervised learning is invaluable for exploratory data analysis and anomaly detection. Customer segmentation in marketing is a prime example, where businesses group customers based on purchasing behavior to tailor marketing strategies. Fraud detection in finance also benefits from unsupervised learning, as algorithms can identify unusual patterns that might indicate fraudulent activity. Unsupervised learning shines in situations where the data lacks labels, and the goal is to uncover inherent structures or anomalies.

Real-world applications further illustrate the versatility of both approaches. In supervised learning, consider a self-driving car that uses labeled data to recognize traffic signs and pedestrians, ensuring safe navigation. Another example is personalized recommendations on streaming platforms, where algorithms learn from your viewing history to suggest new content. On the other hand, unsupervised learning powers recommendation systems that group similar users together, enabling collaborative filtering techniques. It's also used in image compression, where the algorithm reduces the size of image files while retaining important features.

Understanding these two learning methods provides a foundation for grasping how AI systems make sense of data. While supervised learning relies on labeled data to make precise predictions, unsupervised learning explores unlabeled data to find hidden patterns. Both methods have unique strengths and applications, making them essential tools in the AI toolbox. Whether predicting outcomes or uncovering insights, these approaches enable AI to make intelligent decisions across various domains.

2.5 REINFORCEMENT LEARNING: HOW MACHINES LEARN FROM REWARDS

Imagine you're playing a video game where you control a character exploring a maze. Each time your character finds a hidden treasure, you earn points. If your character falls into a trap, you lose points. Over time, you learn to navigate the maze more efficiently, seeking out treasures and avoiding traps. This learning process, driven by rewards and penalties, mirrors the principles of reinforcement learning in AI. Reinforcement learning involves an agent, the decision-maker, interacting with an environment and the world in which the agent operates. The agent takes actions or choices available to it and receives rewards and feedback from the environment based on the outcomes of those actions.

In reinforcement learning, agents learn through trial and error, continuously refining their strategies to maximize rewards. This process involves exploration, where the agent tries new actions to discover their effects, and exploitation, where the agent chooses actions that maximize expected rewards based on past experiences. The ultimate goal is reward maximization, achieving the highest cumulative reward over time. It's like training a pet with treats. Initially, the pet tries various behaviors, but over time, it learns to perform the actions that earn it the most treats.

Key algorithms in reinforcement learning, guide this learning process. One such algorithm is Q-learning, which helps the agent learn the value of actions in different states. Imagine you're playing a board game, and you have a strategy guide that tells you the best moves based on your current position on the board. Q-learning creates a similar guide, known as a Q-table, which maps states to actions and their expected rewards. The agent updates this table as it interacts with the environment, improving its strategy over time. Another important algorithm is policy gradients, which directly optimize the agent's policy—the strategy it uses to decide actions. Think of policy gradients as refining your intuition about which moves are best, based on continuous feedback.

Reinforcement learning has found applications in various real-world scenarios. In game playing, AI agents have achieved superhuman performance in games like chess and Go, where the agents learn complex strategies through countless simulations. For example, AlphaGo, developed by DeepMind, defeated the world champion Go player by learning from millions of game simulations. In robotics, reinforcement learning trains robots to perform complex tasks such as assembling products or navigating unfamiliar environments. These robots learn to optimize their movements and adapt to changing conditions, much like how a human might learn a new skill through practice.

Autonomous driving is another area where reinforcement learning plays a crucial role. Self-driving cars use reinforcement learning to optimize driving strategies, such as navigating traffic, making lane changes, and avoiding obstacles. These cars continuously learn from their experiences on the road, improving their performance and safety over time. Imagine a car learning to drive in a new city; through trial and error, it becomes adept at handling the unique traffic patterns and road conditions of that city.

Reinforcement learning's ability to learn from interactions and improve over time makes it a powerful tool for developing intelligent systems that can adapt to dynamic environments. By understanding the basics of reinforcement learning, the learning process, key algorithms, and real-world applications, you gain insight into how AI systems can achieve remarkable feats through the simple yet effective mechanism of learning from rewards.

As we conclude this chapter, keep in mind that the concepts covered here—machine learning, neural networks, data, and reinforcement learning—are the building blocks of AI. They provide the foundation for understanding how AI systems learn, adapt, and make decisions. In the next chapter, we'll explore the tools and technologies that make AI accessible to beginners, empowering you to apply these concepts in practical ways.

INTERACTIVE QUIZ: CORE CONCEPTS AND
MECHANISMS

1. Understanding Machine Learning

Question: What is machine learning?

    a) A system that only works with predefined rules
    b) A type of artificial intelligence that enables computers to
learn from data without being explicitly programmed
    c) A type of neural network that processes information

- **Question**: Which of the following is an example of
supervised learning?

    a) Grouping customers based on purchasing behavior
    b) Teaching an AI to recognize cats and dogs using labeled
images
    c) Detecting unusual patterns in financial transactions
without prior labels

2. Exploring Neural Networks

- **Question**: What is the primary function of the hidden
layers in a neural network?

    a) To receive input data
    b) To process data through complex computations
    c) To deliver the final output

- **Question**: Which type of neural network is specialized for image recognition tasks?

a) Recurrent Neural Networks (RNNs)
b) Convolutional Neural Networks (CNNs)
c) Feedforward Neural Networks

3. Data in AI

- **Question**: What is structured data?

a) Data stored in databases with rows and columns
b) Text documents and social media posts
c) Data that does not have any clear format

- **Question**: Why is data quality important in AI?

a) To ensure the data is structured
b) To allow the AI system to make accurate predictions
c) To increase the size of the dataset

4. Supervised vs. Unsupervised Learning

- **Question**: In supervised learning, what role do labels play?

a) They provide the AI with different data inputs
b) They are used to identify patterns without guidance
c) They pair each example with the correct output during training

- **Question**: Which learning method is best suited for exploratory data analysis?

  a) Supervised learning
  b) Unsupervised learning
  c) Reinforcement learning

5. Reinforcement Learning

- **Question**: What is the main goal of reinforcement learning?

  a) To minimize data input
  b) To maximize cumulative rewards over time
  c) To classify data into different categories

- **Question**: Which real-world application of reinforcement learning involves training AI to achieve superhuman performance?

  a) Image recognition in smartphones
  b) Game-playing AI like AlphaGo
  c) Analyzing social media trends

3

TOOLS AND TECHNOLOGIES

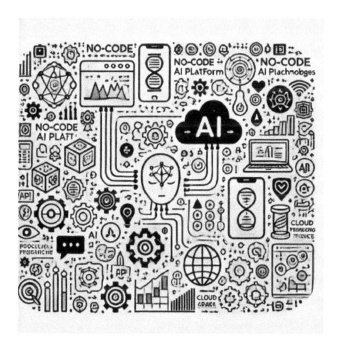

I magine you want to create a smart assistant that can recommend books based on your reading habits. You're excited about the possibilities but are intimidated by the thought of coding. Enter no-code AI platforms, designed to democratize AI by making it accessible to everyone, regardless of their technical background. These platforms allow you to build and deploy AI models without writing a single line of code. Instead of wrestling with programming languages, you can focus on what truly matters: the innovative ideas you want to bring to life.

No-code AI platforms are revolutionizing how we interact with AI by providing user-friendly interfaces and powerful features. They offer drag-and-drop functionality, where you can simply select the components you need and arrange them visually. Imagine building a model like assembling a puzzle; each piece represents a different function, and you can see how they fit together in real-time. These platforms also come with pre-built templates and models, allowing you to jumpstart your projects. Whether you're creating a sentiment analysis tool for social media or developing an image recognition system for quality control, these templates provide a solid foundation.

Another standout feature is automated data preprocessing. Data is the lifeblood of AI, but cleaning and preparing it can be a tedious task. No-code platforms handle this for you, ensuring your data is in the best possible shape for training your models. They also integrate seamlessly with other tools and services, making it easy to pull in data from various sources or export your results to other applications. This interoperability means you can build complex AI systems without worrying about technical compatibility issues.

Several no-code AI platforms have gained popularity for their ease of use and robust capabilities. Google AutoML, for example, allows you to create custom machine learning models tailored to your specific needs. With its intuitive interface, you can train models without needing to understand the intricacies of machine learning algorithms. Microsoft Azure AI offers a comprehensive suite of tools that cater to both beginners and advanced users, making it a versatile choice for a wide range of projects. DataRobot is another powerful platform known for its automated machine learning capabilities, helping you create high-quality models with minimal effort. Lobe by Microsoft stands out for its simplicity, designed to help anyone, regardless of their technical skills, build AI models quickly and effectively.

These platforms have practical applications across various industries. For example, you can use a no-code AI platform to build a customer churn prediction model in retail. By analyzing customer data, the model can identify patterns that indicate when a customer is likely to leave, allowing businesses to take proactive measures to retain them. In social media, you can create a sentiment analysis tool that scans posts and comments to gauge public opinion on different topics. This can be invaluable for brands looking to understand how consumers perceive their products.

Manufacturing is another field where no-code AI platforms shine. Imagine developing an image recognition system that ensures quality control on a production line. The system can automatically detect defects in products, reducing the need for manual inspections and increasing efficiency. These examples illustrate how no-code AI platforms empower you to harness the power of AI without getting bogged down by technical complexities.

Try It Yourself: Building a Sentiment Analysis Tool

1. **Choose a No-Code AI Platform**: Select a platform like Google AutoML or Lobe.
2. **Collect Data**: Gather social media posts or customer reviews related to your topic.
3. **Upload and Preprocess Data**: Use the platform's automated tools to clean and prepare your data.

4. **Build Your Model**: Utilize the drag-and-drop interface to create your sentiment analysis model.
5. **Train and Test**: Train the model with your data and test its accuracy.
6. **Deploy**: Once satisfied, deploy your model to start analyzing real-time data.

No-code AI platforms make AI accessible and approachable for everyone. By breaking down barriers, they allow you to focus on innovation rather than technical hurdles. Whether you're a business owner, a student, or someone with a great idea, these tools provide a gateway to the transformative power of AI.

3.1 AI-POWERED APPS: EVERYDAY TOOLS FOR BEGINNERS

Imagine waking up and checking your phone to find your daily schedule neatly organized, with reminders to drink water and a suggestion for your morning workout. AI-powered apps make this seamless experience possible. These apps integrate advanced technologies like machine learning, natural language processing, and computer vision to enhance functionality and user experience. They also analyze your habits, preferences, and needs to offer intelligent features and insights that make your daily life more efficient and enjoyable.

AI-powered apps come in various categories, each serving a unique purpose. Productivity apps, for example, help you organize your tasks and manage your time effectively. Health and fitness apps keep track of your physical activities, monitor your diet, and provide personalized workout plans. Finance and budgeting apps assist in managing your finances, offering insights into your spending habits and helping you save money. Entertainment and media apps enhance your leisure time by recommending movies, music, and other content based on your interests. These categories showcase the versatility of AI-powered apps in catering to different aspects of your life.

Several AI-powered apps have gained popularity for their user-friendly interfaces and practical benefits. Grammarly is an excellent example of an AI-powered writing assistant. It helps you write more effectively by providing real-time grammar and style suggestions, making your emails, reports, and social media posts polished and professional. MyFitnessPal is another widely-used app that leverages AI to track your fitness and nutrition. It offers personalized recommendations based on your goals, helping you stay on track with your health and fitness journey. PocketGuard is an AI-based personal finance management app that analyzes your spending patterns, helping you create budgets and save money effortlessly. Prisma, an AI-enhanced photo editing app, transforms your photos into stunning works of art with just a few taps, making it easy for anyone to create visually appealing images.

To get the most out of AI-powered apps, consider these practical tips. Start by setting up personalized goals and recommendations. Most AI-powered apps allow you to customize settings based on your preferences and objectives. For example, in a fitness app, you can set specific weight loss goals or workout targets. Utilize the AI insights provided by these apps to make better decisions. For instance, a finance app might highlight unnecessary expenses, helping you cut costs and save more effectively. Explore advanced features and integrations to enhance your experience further. Many AI-powered apps offer additional functionalities that can be unlocked through premium subscriptions or by connecting with other apps and services. This can provide a more comprehensive and tailored experience.

Try It Yourself: Setting Up Personalized Goals

1. **Choose an AI-powered app:** Select an app like MyFitnessPal or PocketGuard.
2. **Create an Account:** Sign up and complete your profile.
3. **Set Your Goals:** Define your fitness, nutrition, or financial goals within the app.
4. **Explore Features:** Familiarize yourself with the app's features, such as daily reminders and progress tracking.
5. **Monitor Your Progress:** Use the app regularly to track your achievements and adjust your goals as needed.

AI-powered apps are designed to simplify and enhance various aspects of your life. By leveraging the power of AI, these apps provide personalized insights and recommendations that help you make informed decisions, stay organized, and achieve your goals. Whether you're looking to improve your productivity, manage your health, or enjoy your leisure time, AI-powered apps offer practical solutions that cater to your unique needs and preferences.

3.2 VISUAL PROGRAMMING WITH AI: TOOLS AND TECHNIQUES

Imagine you're trying to create an AI model but feel overwhelmed by the thought of writing complex code. Visual programming offers a solution by allowing you to build programs using graphical elements. Rather than typing lines of code, you manipulate visual objects on the screen, making the process more intuitive and accessible. Think of it as assembling a Lego set where each block represents a different function or operation. This approach significantly lowers the barrier to entry, especially for beginners who are new to AI and programming.

Several visual programming tools have become popular for AI development due to their user-friendly interfaces and powerful capabilities. Scratch, for instance, is a beginner-friendly visual programming language often used in educational settings. It allows users to create interactive stories, games, and animations by snapping together code blocks like puzzle pieces. Node-RED, another tool, is a flow-based development environment that lets you wire devices, APIs, and online services together. Its drag-and-drop interface makes it easy to create complex workflows without writing code. IBM Watson Studio offers visual modeling tools specifically designed for AI development, enabling users to build, train, and deploy machine learning models through an intuitive, graphical interface.

Creating AI models using visual programming tools involves a straightforward, step-by-step process. First, you start by dragging and dropping components from a palette onto your workspace. Each component represents a different function, such as data input, processing, or output. Next, you connect these components to define the data flow, similar to drawing a flowchart. This visual representation helps you see how data moves through the system, making it easier to understand and debug. After that, you set parameters and configurations for each component. For example, you might specify the type of algorithm to use or the size of the training dataset. Finally, you run and test your model to evaluate its performance. If the results aren't satisfactory, you can easily go back and tweak the configurations or adjust the data flow.

Visual programming tools are versatile and can be used to develop a wide range of AI applications. For instance, you can create a simple chatbot that can answer frequently asked questions. You can build a functional chatbot without writing a single line of code by dragging and connecting blocks that handle text input, processing, and output. Another example is developing an AI-based recommendation system. You can use visual programming to analyze user preferences and suggest products or content tailored to individual tastes. If you're interested in image recognition, you can build an image classification model by configuring blocks that handle image data, train a neural network, and output the classification results. These examples show how visual programming tools empower you to create sophisticated AI applications in an accessible and intuitive way.

3.3 AI IN THE CLOUD: LEVERAGING CLOUD-BASED AI SERVICES

Imagine you're a small business owner with a brilliant idea for an AI-driven customer service chatbot. However, the thought of investing in expensive hardware and infrastructure feels overwhelming. This is where cloud-based AI services come into play. These services provide scalable, on-demand access to AI tools and resources, eliminating the need for extensive hardware. Essentially, they allow you to tap into powerful AI capabilities through the internet, making advanced technology accessible without hefty upfront costs.

Leading the charge in cloud-based AI services are major providers like Amazon Web Services (AWS), Google Cloud AI, Microsoft Azure AI, and IBM Cloud AI. Each offers a suite of AI tools designed to cater to various needs. AWS AI Services, for instance, provide everything from machine learning and natural language processing to computer vision. Google Cloud AI stands out with its robust set of APIs and pre-built models, making it a favorite among developers. Microsoft Azure AI offers comprehensive tools and frameworks, including Azure Machine Learning, for building and deploying models. IBM Cloud AI also provides a range of services with a strong focus on enterprise solutions and integration capabilities.

Getting started with these cloud AI services is straightforward and user-friendly. Begin by creating an account on your chosen cloud platform. Once registered, you'll find a service dashboard that serves as your control center, guiding you through available tools and resources. Selecting pre-built AI models can significantly speed up your project, as these models are trained on vast datasets and fine-tuned for specific tasks. Deploying and scaling AI solutions is also simplified. You can start with a small-scale deployment to test your model and then scale up as needed, ensuring you only pay for what you use.

Real-world examples highlight the transformative potential of cloud-based AI services across various industries. In retail, AI-powered personalized shopping experiences can analyze customer behavior to recommend products, increasing sales and customer satisfaction. Healthcare providers use predictive analytics to anticipate patient needs and improve treatment outcomes. For instance, AI models can predict the likelihood of readmission for patients, allowing for proactive interventions. In finance, AI-driven fraud detection systems analyze transaction patterns to identify suspicious activities, protecting both businesses and consumers. Manufacturing companies leverage AI for predictive maintenance, using data from machinery to predict and prevent equipment failures, thereby reducing downtime and costs.

These cloud-based AI services open up a world of possibilities, enabling you to integrate AI into your projects without the barrier of high costs or technical complexity. Whether you're enhancing customer experiences, improving healthcare, safeguarding financial transactions, or optimizing manufacturing processes, cloud AI services provide the tools you need to innovate and succeed.

3.4 OPEN-SOURCE AI: EXPLORING FREE AND POWERFUL RESOURCES

Imagine you're sitting at your computer, excited to dive into AI but hesitant about the costs and accessibility of the tools you might need. This is where open-source AI steps in, offering a world of possibilities without the hefty price tag. Open-source AI involves publicly available tools, frameworks, and libraries that anyone can use, modify, and share. This openness fosters innovation and collaboration, allowing developers and enthusiasts from around the globe to contribute to and benefit from advancements in AI technology. It's like a global community where everyone shares their recipes, improving them together for the greater good.

One of the most widely used open-source AI frameworks is TensorFlow, developed by Google. TensorFlow is a comprehensive machine learning framework that supports a wide range of applications, from simple linear regression to complex neural networks. It's like having a Swiss Army knife for AI, equipped with tools for any task you might encounter. PyTorch, another popular framework, is known for its flexibility and ease of use. Developed by Facebook, PyTorch is favored by researchers and developers alike for its dynamic computation graph, which makes it easier to debug and experiment with new ideas. Scikit-learn is a library specifically designed for data mining and data analysis. It provides simple and efficient tools for predictive data analysis, making it a favorite among data scientists. Keras, an easy-to-use neural network library, acts as a high-level API for TensorFlow, simplifying the process of building and training deep learning models.

Getting started with these open-source AI tools is straightforward, even for beginners. For instance, you can install TensorFlow using pip, a package manager for Python. A simple command in your terminal—pip install TensorFlow—and you're ready to go.

Building and training a neural network with Keras also involves just a few lines of code. You define your model, compile it, and then train it on your data. It's like assembling a model airplane; the instructions are clear, and the pieces fit together seamlessly. Performing data analysis with Scikit-learn is equally intuitive. With functions for data preprocessing, model selection, and evaluation, Scikit-learn provides a streamlined workflow from start to finish.

The open-source AI community is a vital resource for support and collaboration. Participating in online forums and discussion groups allows you to ask questions, share insights, and learn from others' experiences. Websites like Stack Overflow and Reddit have active communities where you can find answers to almost any problem you encounter. Contributing to open-source projects on GitHub is another way to get involved. By working on existing projects or starting your own, you gain practical experience and connect with other developers. Accessing tutorials and documentation is also crucial. Most open-source libraries come with extensive documentation and tutorials, guiding you through the basics to more advanced concepts. Joining AI meetups and conferences can further enhance your learning experience. These events provide opportunities to network with professionals, attend workshops, and stay updated on the latest trends in AI.

Community Engagement: Join the Conversation

1. **Find Online Forums:** Platforms like Stack Overflow and Reddit are great starting places.
2. **Contribute to GitHub:** Look for open-source projects that interest you and start contributing.
3. **Attend Meetups and Conferences:** Check for local AI meetups or virtual conferences.

4. **Explore Tutorials:** Use online tutorials and documentation to deepen your understanding.

Engaging with the open-source AI community enhances your skills and provides a support network to help you navigate challenges. The collaborative nature of open-source projects means you're never alone in your journey. Whether you're troubleshooting an issue or looking for new ideas, there's always someone out there willing to lend a hand.

Interactive Quiz: Tools and Technologies

1. No-Code AI Platforms

- **Question**: What is the primary benefit of using no-code AI platforms?

  a) They eliminate the need to write code, making AI accessible to non-technical users
  b) They are only for advanced programmers
  c) They require extensive knowledge of data preprocessing techniques

- **Question**: Which of the following is a popular no-code AI platform?

  a) Scratch
  b) Google AutoML
  c) TensorFlow

2. AI-Powered Apps

- **Question**: What is the main function of AI-powered productivity apps?

a) Entertaining users with games
b) Organizing tasks and managing time efficiently
c) Editing photos with filters

- **Question**: Which app is an AI-powered writing assistant that offers grammar and style suggestions?

a) MyFitnessPal
b) PocketGuard
c) Grammarly

3. Visual Programming for AI

- **Question**: What is visual programming?

a) A type of programming that uses graphical elements instead of code
b) A coding language for AI experts
c) A text-based coding environment

- **Question**: Which visual programming tool is commonly used for building AI models with a drag-and-drop interface?

a) IBM Watson Studio
b) Google Cloud AI
c) AWS AI Services

4. Cloud-Based AI Services

- **Question**: What is one advantage of using cloud-based AI services?

  a) You must own expensive hardware to use them
  b) They provide scalable, on-demand access to AI tools without high upfront costs
  c) They are only available to large corporations

- **Question**: Which cloud provider offers Azure AI for building and deploying machine learning models?

  a) Amazon Web Services (AWS)
  b) Microsoft
  c) IBM

5. Open-Source AI Tools

- **Question**: What is TensorFlow?

  a) A proprietary AI framework
  b) An open-source AI framework developed by Google
  c) An AI hardware platform

- **Question**: Which open-source AI library is specifically designed for data analysis and predictive modeling?

  a) PyTorch
  b) Scikit-learn
  c) Keras

4

PRACTICAL APPLICATIO

Imagine walking into a hospital where a doctor greets you with a stethoscope and a tablet powered by Artificial Intelligence (AI). This is not a scene from a futuristic movie but a glimpse into the evolving healthcare landscape. AI is revolutionizing how we diagnose and treat diseases, making healthcare more efficient, accurate, and personalized. From analyzing medical images to predicting patient outcomes, AI is transforming the medical field in ways we are only beginning to appreciate.

4.1 AI IN HEALTHCARE: REVOLUTIONIZING DIAGNOSIS AND TREATMENT

AI in medical imaging is one of the most groundbreaking applications transforming healthcare today. Imagine a radiologist examining an MRI scan to detect a tumor. Traditionally, this process relied heavily on the radiologist's experience and keen eye. However, with AI algorithms, the accuracy and speed of diagnosis have significantly improved. These algorithms can analyze medical images such as MRI and CT scans far more quickly than a human can. They're trained on thousands of images to recognize patterns and anomalies, making them exceptionally good at identifying issues the human eye might miss. For example, AI has been used to detect tumors, ensuring early diagnosis and treatment, which is crucial for patient outcomes. Similarly, in the field of ophthalmology, AI algorithms can identify diabetic retinopathy in retinal images, a condition that can lead to blindness if not caught early. These advancements mean patients receive quicker, more accurate diagnoses, leading to timely and effective treatments.

Predictive analytics is another area where AI is making significant strides. Picture a scenario where a hospital can predict which patients will most likely be readmitted after discharge. By analyzing historical data and patient records, AI can identify patterns that signal a higher risk of readmission. This allows healthcare providers to implement preventive measures, such as follow-up appointments and personalized care plans, reducing the likelihood of readmission. In oncology, AI is being used to personalize cancer treatment plans based on genetic data. Each patient's cancer is unique, and a one-size-fits-all approach is often ineffective. AI can analyze genetic information to determine which treatments are most likely to be effective for a particular patient, tailoring therapies to their specific needs. This personalized approach improves treatment outcomes and reduces unnecessary side effects.

AI-powered virtual health assistants are transforming patient engagement and care. Imagine having a virtual assistant that can answer your health-related queries 24/7. AI chatbots can answer common questions accurately, helping patients manage their health more effectively. These virtual assistants can also offer symptom checkers, guiding patients on whether they need to seek medical attention or can manage their symptoms at home. This immediate access to information can benefit those living in remote areas with limited healthcare services. Moreover, these virtual assistants can remind patients to take their medications, schedule appointments, and monitor their health metrics, ensuring continuous care and engagement.

The drug discovery and development process, traditionally a lengthy and costly endeavor, is being accelerated by AI. Imagine the time and resources required to bring a new drug to market, years of research, countless experiments, and millions of dollars. AI is streamlining this process by identifying potential drug candidates more quickly and accurately. By analyzing vast datasets, AI can pinpoint compounds that are likely to be effective against specific diseases, significantly speeding up the initial stages of drug discovery. Furthermore, AI can simulate drug interactions, predict potential side effects, and optimize dosages before clinical trials begin. This reduces the time and cost involved and increases the likelihood of success in later stages of development.

Interactive Element: Case Study Analysis

Case Study: AI in Oncology

Read the following scenario and reflect on the questions below.

Dr. Smith, an oncologist, uses an AI system to analyze genetic data from her patients. The AI identifies a specific genetic marker that suggests a higher likelihood of responding to a new immunotherapy drug. Based on this insight, Dr. Smith tailors the treatment plan for her patient, significantly improving the patient's condition.

Reflection Questions:

1. How did AI contribute to the personalized treatment plan in this case?
2. What are the potential benefits and challenges of using AI in personalized medicine?

By integrating AI into healthcare, we are witnessing a transformation that promises to improve patient outcomes, streamline operations, and make medical care more accessible and effective. From enhancing diagnostic accuracy to personalizing treatments and accelerating drug discovery, AI is poised to revolutionize the healthcare industry in profound ways.

4.2 AI IN FINANCE: ENHANCING SECURITY AND PREDICTIVE ANALYTICS

Imagine you're making an online purchase, and within seconds, your bank flags the transaction as suspicious. This is thanks to AI-driven fraud detection systems working tirelessly to protect your financial well-being. AI algorithms analyze vast amounts of transaction data in real time, identifying patterns that indicate fraudu-lent activities. For example, if someone tries to use your credit card in two different countries within hours, AI can quickly detect this anomaly and alert you. These systems are trained to recognize unusual spending behaviors, such as multiple small purchases followed by a large one, a common tactic fraudsters use. By continuously learning from new data, AI systems become more adept at spotting and preventing fraud, ensuring your transactions are secure.

In the investment world, AI is transforming how financial deci-sions are made. Predictive analytics plays a crucial role in helping investors navigate the complexities of the market. AI algorithms sift through vast amounts of financial data, from stock prices and trading volumes to news articles and social media sentiment. AI can predict market trends and inform investment strategies by analyzing this information. Imagine using an AI-driven invest-ment recommendation system that suggests stocks based on current market conditions and historical data. These systems can even analyze market sentiment by scanning news headlines and social media posts, providing insights into investors' feelings about particular stocks or sectors. This allows you to make informed decisions, reducing the guesswork and increasing the likelihood of profitable investments.

AI-powered chatbots have also revolutionized customer service in financial institutions. Picture yourself needing assistance with your bank account late at night. Instead of waiting for business hours, you can interact with an AI chatbot that's available 24/7. These chatbots can handle various inquiries, from checking your account balance to transferring funds. They are designed to understand natural language, making the interaction feel more intuitive and less robotic. Additionally, AI-driven virtual assistants can provide personalized financial advice, helping you manage your budget, track expenses, and even plan for future investments. This level of personalized service enhances customer satisfaction and builds trust in financial institutions.

Risk management is another critical area where AI is making a significant impact. Traditional financial risk assessment methods often rely on static models and historical data. AI, however, brings a dynamic approach to risk management. AI can provide more accurate and timely risk assessments by analyzing real-time data and identifying emerging trends. For example, AI algorithms used in credit scoring can analyze a broader range of factors, such as spending habits and social media activity, to determine creditworthiness. This results in more accurate credit scores and better loan approval decisions. In assessing financial risks, predictive models powered by AI can identify potential market downturns or economic shifts, allowing financial institutions to take proactive measures to mitigate risks.

Interactive Element: Risk Assessment Exercise

Exercise: AI in Risk Management

Use the following steps to simulate an AI-driven risk assessment for a hypothetical loan application.

1. Gather Data: Collect data on the applicant, including credit score, income, employment history, and spending habits.
2. Analyze Patterns: Use an AI tool to analyze patterns in the data, identifying risk factors such as irregular income or high debt-to-income ratio.
3. Predict Outcomes: Based on the analysis, predict the likelihood of loan default.

4. Make a Decision: Decide whether to approve or deny the loan, providing reasons based on the AI's assessment.

As you can see, AI's role in finance is multifaceted. It enhances security, improves investment strategies, revolutionizes customer service, and refines risk management practices. By leveraging the power of AI, financial institutions can offer better services, make more informed decisions, and provide a higher level of security and personalization to their customers.

4.3 AI IN RETAIL: PERSONALIZING SHOPPING EXPERIENCES

Imagine strolling through your favorite online store. As you browse, a section with "Recommended for You" appears, showcasing products that seem to align perfectly with your tastes. This isn't a coincidence but the work of AI-powered recommendation engines. These engines analyze your browsing history, purchase patterns, and even the time spent on specific items. By processing this data, AI can predict what products might catch your interest next. For example, if you frequently buy fitness gear, the recommendation engine will prioritize showing you the latest in athletic wear or gym equipment. This personalized experience makes shopping more enjoyable and efficient, aligning the store's offerings with your unique preferences.

AI also plays a crucial role in tailoring marketing messages to individual preferences. Picture receiving an email from an e-commerce platform that addresses you by name features, products, and deals that match your previous purchases. AI algorithms analyze customer data to segment audiences and deliver personalized marketing campaigns. This means that the promotional emails or app notifications you receive are crafted specifically for you, increasing the likelihood of engagement and conversion. By understanding your preferences, AI helps retailers create a more personalized and appealing shopping experience, enhancing customer satisfaction and loyalty.

Efficient inventory management is another area where AI proves invaluable. Imagine a retailer anticipating high demand for a new product launch. Using AI, the retailer can predict demand and optimize stock levels, ensuring they have enough inventory to meet customer needs without overstocking. AI analyzes historical sales data, current market trends, and even factors like seasonal fluctuations to make accurate predictions. Automated restocking systems further streamline this process by continuously monitoring inventory levels and triggering orders when stock runs low. This reduces the risk of stockouts and minimizes carrying costs, making the supply chain more efficient and responsive.

Customer service in retail has been transformed by AI, enhancing how queries and complaints are handled. Think about the last time you needed assistance on an e-commerce site. Chances are, an AI chatbot was there to help. These chatbots can handle various customer queries, from tracking orders to processing returns. They are designed to understand natural language, making interactions smooth and intuitive. Virtual shopping assistants take this a step further by offering personalized recommendations and helping customers navigate the website. By providing instant, 24/7 support, AI chatbots improve customer satisfaction and free up human agents to handle more complex issues.

AI is also revolutionizing in-store shopping experiences. Imagine walking into a store and using an AI-powered smart mirror to try on clothes virtually. These mirrors use augmented reality to superimpose clothing items onto your reflection, allowing you to see how different outfits look without physically trying them on.

This not only saves time but also enhances the shopping experience. AI is also used to analyze customer behavior and preferences within the store. For example, cameras equipped with computer vision can monitor foot traffic and identify popular areas. This data helps retailers optimize store layouts and product placements, ensuring customers a more enjoyable and efficient shopping experience.

AI's integration into retail is about convenience and creating a more personalized and engaging shopping experience. By analyzing vast amounts of data, AI can predict customers' wants, manage inventory efficiently, provide exceptional customer service, and enhance in-store experiences. This blend of technology and retail creates a seamless shopping journey, making each interaction more meaningful and tailored to individual needs. As AI continues to evolve, its impact on retail will only grow, offering even more innovative ways to enhance how we shop.

4.4 AI IN TRANSPORTATION: THE ROAD TO AUTONOMOUS VEHICLES

Imagine sitting in a car that drives itself while you read a book or catch up on emails. This is the vision of autonomous vehicles, a technology rapidly becoming a reality. Self-driving cars use AI to navigate roads, make real-time decisions, and ensure passenger safety. These vehicles are equipped with sensors and cameras that capture their surroundings, feeding data into sophisticated AI algorithms. These algorithms process the data to identify objects, predict movements, and control the car's actions. For example, AI systems in autonomous vehicles can detect pedestrians and cyclists, predict their paths, and adjust speed or direction to avoid collisions. Safety features like automatic braking and lane-keeping assistance further enhance the driving experience, making roads safer for everyone.

AI is also revolutionizing traffic management, making our commutes more efficient. Picture a city with smart traffic lights that adjust their timing based on real-time traffic conditions. These AI-driven systems can predict traffic flow and reduce congestion by optimizing signal timings. For instance, smart traffic lights can extend green signals on busier roads during rush hour to alleviate traffic jams. AI also plays a crucial role in dynamic routing for public transportation. Buses and trains can adjust their routes and schedules based on current traffic conditions and passenger demand. This reduces travel time and improves the overall efficiency of public transport systems, making them more reliable and attractive to commuters.

In vehicle maintenance, AI is proving to be a game-changer. Imagine your car alerting you to a potential issue before it becomes a major problem. AI systems can monitor vehicle performance in real time, analyzing data from various sensors to detect anomalies. For example, if the AI detects an unusual vibration or temperature spike, it can predict a component failure and schedule maintenance before a breakdown occurs. This predictive maintenance approach reduces downtime and repair costs, ensuring that vehicles remain in optimal condition. Fleet operators, in particular, benefit from this technology, as it allows them to maintain large numbers of vehicles more efficiently, minimizing disruptions and enhancing operational reliability.

Ride-sharing services and logistics operations also reap the benefits of AI. Think about how ride-sharing apps like Uber and Lyft have transformed urban mobility. AI algorithms optimize routes, matching drivers with passengers in real time to minimize waiting times and fuel consumption. These systems analyze traffic patterns, weather conditions, and demand forecasts to provide the most efficient routes. In logistics, AI is streamlining delivery services by optimizing fleet management. For instance, delivery companies use AI to plan routes that reduce travel time and fuel costs. AI can also predict delays and adjust schedules accordingly, ensuring timely deliveries. This efficiency not only improves customer satisfaction but also reduces the environmental impact of transportation.

Interactive Element: AI in Your Commute

Exercise: Visualize AI's Impact on Your Daily Commute

1. Current Commute: Write down the typical challenges you face during your daily commute.
2. AI Enhancements: Imagine how AI could address these challenges. Consider aspects like traffic management, vehicle maintenance, and route optimization.
3. Future Commute: Describe your ideal commute with AI enhancements. How does it improve your experience?

By integrating AI into transportation, we are on the brink of a mobility revolution. Autonomous vehicles promise safer and more convenient travel, while AI-driven traffic management can ease congestion. Predictive maintenance ensures that vehicles are always in top condition, and ride-sharing services become more efficient with AI's help. These advancements are not just about convenience; they have the potential to transform how we move, making our journeys safer, faster, and more sustainable.

4.5 AI IN CREATIVE FIELDS: GENERATING ART, MUSIC, AND WRITING

Picture a gallery filled with stunning paintings, each one more captivating than the last. Some of these artworks were not crafted by human hands but by AI algorithms. AI-generated art is making waves in the art world, challenging our perceptions of creativity and authorship. Algorithms analyze thousands of images to learn styles, techniques, and patterns. They then generate original pieces that can be indistinguishable from human-created art. For instance, an AI might produce a digital painting that mimics the brushstrokes of Van Gogh or the abstract forms of Picasso. Some artists collaborate with AI, using it as a tool to explore new creative directions. These collaborations push the boundaries of what's possible, blending human intuition with machine precision to create something entirely new.

AI is proving to be a virtuoso composer in the realm of music. Imagine listening to a piece of music that moves you deeply, only to learn it was composed by an AI. AI tools are now capable of composing original music pieces, generating melodies, harmonies, and even full orchestral arrangements. These systems analyze vast collections of music to understand the structure, rhythm, and emotional tone of different genres. Musicians can use AI to generate ideas, create backing tracks, or even produce entire compositions. This doesn't mean AI is replacing human musicians; rather, it's becoming a powerful tool that enhances musical creativity. AI can suggest chord progressions, refine melodies, and offer new perspectives, allowing musicians to focus on the emotional and expressive aspects of their craft.

AI is also transforming writing and content creation. Picture a writer working on an article with an AI tool suggesting improvements in real time. AI can draft articles, stories, and even poetry, analyzing vast amounts of text to generate coherent and engaging content. These tools can assist writers by suggesting sentence structures, refining grammar, and enhancing style. For example, an AI might help a journalist by quickly drafting a news report based on data inputs, allowing the journalist to focus on adding human insights and context. AI can also aid in editing, catching errors that human eyes might miss, and ensuring that the final piece is polished and professional. This partnership between human writers and AI can produce higher-quality content more efficiently.

However, the rise of AI-generated content brings ethical considerations and questions of originality to the forefront. One major debate revolves around the authorship of AI-generated work. If an AI creates a painting or composes a piece of music, who owns the rights to that work? Is it the programmer who designed the algorithm, the user who input the data, or the AI itself? These questions challenge our traditional notions of creativity and intellectual property. Ethical guidelines are being developed to navigate these complexities, ensuring that AI is used responsibly in creative fields. There's also the concern of authenticity: can AI-generated art truly capture the depth of human experience? While AI can mimic styles and generate aesthetically pleasing works, some argue that it lacks the emotional depth and intentionality that define human creativity.

As we explore the vast potential of AI in creative fields, it's clear that this technology is not just a tool but a collaborator. AI offers new possibilities for artists, musicians, and writers, enabling them to push the boundaries of their craft and explore uncharted territories. Whether generating art, composing music, or aiding in writing, AI is becoming integral to the creative process, opening up new avenues for expression and innovation.

AI's impact on various sectors is profound and wide-ranging. From healthcare to finance, retail, transportation, and creative fields, AI is transforming how we live, work, and create. Each application offers unique benefits and challenges, shaping the future in ways we are only beginning to understand. In the next chapter, we will delve into hands-on projects that will allow you to apply what you've learned and explore AI's practical applications further.

Interactive Quiz: Practical Applications

1. AI in Healthcare

- **Question**: How is AI improving medical imaging analysis?

  a) By replacing radiologists entirely
  b) By identifying patterns and anomalies in medical images faster and more accurately than humans
  c) By focusing only on physical symptoms without data analysis

- **Question**: What is one benefit of using AI in predictive analytics for healthcare?

  a) Providing one-size-fits-all treatment plans
  b) Predicting which patients are at higher risk for readmission, allowing for proactive care
  c) Reducing personalized care and focusing on generalized data

2. AI in Finance

- **Question**: How does AI contribute to fraud detection in financial transactions?

  a) By manually reviewing every transaction
  b) By analyzing transaction patterns in real-time to detect unusual behavior
  c) By only monitoring large transactions

- **Question**: Which of these applications uses AI to provide personalized financial advice and manage customer inquiries?

  a) Investment funds
  b) AI-powered chatbots
  c) Paper-based financial reports

3. AI in Retail

- **Question**: How do AI-powered recommendation engines enhance the shopping experience?

  a) By suggesting random products unrelated to the user's preferences
  b) By analyzing browsing and purchase history to recommend products tailored to individual tastes
  c) By only showing popular products, regardless of user preferences

- **Question**: What role does AI play in inventory management?

a) It randomly stocks products
b) It predicts demand and automates restocking processes based on data analysis
c) It ignores historical data and trends

4. AI in Transportation

- **Question**: How do autonomous vehicles use AI for safe navigation?

a) By ignoring obstacles and driving solely based on maps
b) By using sensors and cameras to detect objects and adjust driving in real-time
c) By relying only on human input

- **Question**: How can AI improve public transportation efficiency?

a) By keeping fixed schedules without adjusting for real-time conditions
b) By dynamically routing buses and trains based on current traffic and demand
c) By focusing solely on reducing costs without considering passengers

5. AI in Creative Fields

- **Question**: What is AI-generated art?

a) Art created by mimicking existing human works without any originality
b) Art created using algorithms that analyze styles and generate new, original pieces
c) Art only created by blending pre-existing images

- **Question**: How is AI used in music composition?

a) By replacing all human musicians
b) By analyzing existing music to generate new melodies and harmonies
c) By creating only monotonous background tracks

5

HANDS-ON PROJECTS

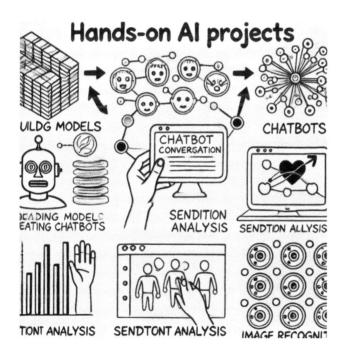

I magine standing in your kitchen, ready to bake a cake for the first time. You have a recipe, ingredients laid out, and a clear vision of the delicious result. This chapter is your recipe for creating your first AI model. Just as you would follow a step-by-step guide to bake that cake, we'll walk through each phase of building a simple machine learning model. By the end, you'll have a model that can predict housing prices based on a dataset, offering you a taste of what AI can achieve.

5.1 BUILDING YOUR FIRST AI MODEL: A STEP-BY-STEP GUIDE

In this project, you will build a machine learning model to predict housing prices. This model will analyze various factors like the number of rooms, location, and other features to estimate the price of a house. By completing this project, you'll gain a foundational understanding of how machine learning models are built, trained, and evaluated. It's a practical, hands-on experience that will demystify AI and show you just how accessible it can be.

The first step in any machine learning project is selecting and preparing a suitable dataset. For this project, we will use the Boston Housing dataset from the UCI Machine Learning Repository. This dataset contains information about various homes in Boston, including features like the number of rooms, crime rate, and distance to employment centers. Before diving into model building, it's crucial to clean and preprocess the data. Start by loading the dataset into a data analysis tool like Python's Pandas library. Check for any missing values and handle them appropriately, either by filling in with a mean value or removing the incomplete rows. Normalize the data to ensure features with different scales don't skew the model's performance. This step is like prepping your ingredients before baking, ensuring everything is measured and ready to go.

Once your data is prepped, it's time to build and train your model. We'll use a linear regression model for this project, as it's straightforward and effective for predicting continuous values like housing prices. Begin by splitting your dataset into training and test sets. The training set will be used to teach the model, while the test set will evaluate its performance. This split ensures the model learns to generalize its predictions to new, unseen data. Next, define your model by specifying the algorithm—linear regression in this case, and train it using the training data. The model will analyze the relationships between the features and the target variable (housing prices) to find the best-fit line that minimizes prediction errors.

With your model trained, the next step is to evaluate its performance. Calculating performance metrics like Mean Squared Error (MSE) will help you understand how well your model is making predictions. MSE measures the average squared difference between the predicted and actual values, providing insight into the model's accuracy. A lower MSE indicates better performance. If the MSE is higher than expected, consider tuning the model's hyperparameters. Hyperparameters are settings that control the training process, such as the learning rate or the number of iterations. Adjusting these settings can improve the model's performance. Additionally, techniques like cross-validation can help assess the model's ability to generalize to new data. Cross-validation involves training multiple models on different subsets of the data and averaging their performance, providing a more robust evaluation.

Interactive Element: Visualize Your Model's Performance

1. Plot Actual vs. Predicted Prices: Create a scatter plot with actual housing prices on the x-axis and predicted prices on the y-axis. This visualization helps you see how well your model's predictions align with the actual values.

2. Analyze Residuals: Plot the residuals (differences between actual and predicted prices) to identify any patterns or outliers. Residual analysis can highlight areas where the model may be underperforming.

3. Compare Performance Metrics: Calculate and compare different performance metrics, such as MSE, Mean Absolute Error (MAE), and R-squared. Each metric provides unique insights into the model's accuracy and reliability.

By following these steps, you'll build a functional machine learning model to predict housing prices, gaining hands-on experience with AI. This project lays the foundation for more complex models and applications, empowering you to explore the vast possibilities of AI.

5.2 CREATING A CHATBOT: PRACTICAL EXERCISE FOR BEGINNERS

Imagine you're on a website, and a small window pops up in the corner, asking if you need help finding what you're looking for. You type in a question, and within seconds, you get a helpful response. This is the magic of chatbots, AI-driven programs that simulate human conversation. They're used across various industries, from customer service to virtual assistants, streamlining interactions, and providing instant support. Chatbots can handle a wide range of tasks, making them invaluable tools for businesses and users alike. Whether it's answering frequently asked questions, booking appointments, or providing personalized recommendations, chatbots are transforming how we interact with technology.

Designing a chatbot starts with defining its purpose and functionality. Begin by choosing a specific use case for your chatbot. For instance, you could create a customer support bot for an online store. Next, outline the chatbot's conversation flow and key inter-actions. Think of it as drafting a script for a play. You'll need to map out a conversation's various paths, including greetings, responses to common queries, and ways to handle more complex questions. This phase is crucial because it sets the foundation for your chatbot's operation. Consider what information the chatbot needs to collect from users and how it will respond to different inputs. For example, if a customer asks about the status of their order, the chatbot should be able to prompt for the order number and provide a status update.

Building the chatbot doesn't require advanced coding skills, thanks to no-code platforms like Dialogflow and Microsoft Bot Framework. Start by signing up for one of these platforms. Once you're in, you'll begin by setting up intents and entities. Intents are the goals or purposes of each user interaction, such as asking for store hours or checking order status. Entities are the pieces of information the chatbot needs to fulfill these intents, like dates, times, or order numbers. For example, you might create an intent called "CheckOrderStatus" and define entities for order numbers and dates. Training the chatbot involves providing sample dialogues or phrases that users might say. This helps the chatbot recognize different ways people might ask the same question. For instance, users might say, "Where's my order?" or "Can you check my order status?" Training your bot with these variations ensures it understands and responds accurately.

Testing and deploying the chatbot is the final phase. Begin by running test conversations to identify and fix any issues. This might involve simulating various user interactions and checking how the chatbot responds. Look for any gaps or errors in the conversation flow and make necessary adjustments. Once you're confident in the chatbot's performance, it's time to deploy it. This could mean integrating it into a website, a messaging platform like Facebook Messenger, or even a mobile app. After deployment, monitor the chatbot's interactions and gather user feedback. This ongoing process helps you refine the chatbot, making it more effective over time. For instance, if users frequently ask questions the bot can't answer, you'll know to update its training data or conversation flow.

Interactive Element: Refining Your Chatbot

1. Simulate Conversations: Take time to simulate various user interactions with your chatbot. Try different phrases and questions to see how the bot responds.
2. Collect Feedback: Gather feedback from real users. Ask them about their experience and any difficulties they encountered.
3. Update Training Data: Use the feedback to update the chatbot's training data. Add new intents and entities as needed to cover more scenarios.
4. Monitor Performance: Regularly check the chatbot's performance metrics, such as response accuracy and user satisfaction. Make ongoing improvements to enhance its functionality.

Creating a chatbot offers a hands-on introduction to AI, making it accessible and engaging. By following these steps, you'll build a functional chatbot and gain insights into how AI can be applied to solve real-world problems.

5.3 SENTIMENT ANALYSIS WITH AI: UNDERSTANDING SOCIAL MEDIA

Imagine scrolling through your favorite social media platform and seeing a flood of posts about a recent product launch. Some users are thrilled, others are disappointed, and many are somewhere in between. Sentiment analysis is a powerful AI tool that helps us decipher the emotional tone behind these posts. By analyzing the text, sentiment analysis can determine whether the overall sentiment is positive, negative, or neutral. This technique is invaluable for businesses, marketers, and researchers who want to gauge public opinion, track brand reputation, and understand consumer behavior. By the end of this project, you'll be able to build a model that analyzes social media sentiments, providing you with insights into how people feel about specific topics.

To get started, you'll need to collect and preprocess social media data. APIs (Application Programming Interfaces) are commonly used to gather data from platforms like Twitter and Facebook. These APIs allow you to extract posts, comments, and other user-generated content for analysis. Once you have your data, cleaning, and preprocessing are the next steps. This involves removing any irrelevant information, such as URLs, hashtags, and special characters. Tokenization is the process of breaking down text into individual words or tokens, making it easier to analyze. You'll also need to remove stop words and common words like "and," "the," and "is," which don't add meaningful information to the analysis. Preprocessing ensures your data is in a suitable format for training your sentiment analysis model.

Building a sentiment analysis model involves selecting and training a classification algorithm with labeled sentiment data. Algorithms like Naive Bayes and Support Vector Machine (SVM) are popular choices for this task. You'll start by splitting your dataset into training and test sets. The training set teaches the model to recognize patterns associated with different sentiments, while the test set evaluates its performance. Labeling the data means categorizing each post as positive, negative, or neutral. This labeled data serves as the foundation for training your model. Once trained, the model can predict the sentiment of new, unlabeled posts. Evaluating the model's performance involves calculating metrics like accuracy and F1 score, which measure how well the model classifies sentiments. A higher accuracy indicates better performance, while the F1 score balances precision and recall.

Applying your trained sentiment analysis model to real-world data involves running it on new social media posts. Start by collecting a fresh dataset of recent tweets or Facebook posts related to a specific topic. Feed this data into your model to analyze the sentiment. You can visualize the results using graphs and charts to see the distribution of sentiments over time. For example, a line graph might show how the sentiment changes before and after a product launch. This visualization helps you interpret the insights and understand public sentiment on specific topics. Analyzing these results can reveal trends, such as increasing negative sentiments following a controversial event or growing positive sentiments around a successful campaign.

Interactive Element: Sentiment Analysis in Action

1. Collect Data: Use APIs to gather social media posts about a recent event or product launch.
2. Preprocess Text: Clean the text data by removing irrelevant information, tokenizing, and eliminating stop words.
3. Train Model: Choose a classification algorithm, label your data, and train your sentiment analysis model.

4. Visualize Results: Create graphs and charts to visualize the sentiment distribution and identify trends.
5. Interpret Insights: Analyze the visualizations to understand public sentiment and draw actionable conclusions.

Sentiment analysis offers a fascinating glimpse into how people express their emotions online. By building and applying your own sentiment analysis model, you'll gain practical experience with AI and uncover valuable insights from social media data. This project enhances your understanding of AI and equips you with the skills to analyze and interpret complex datasets.

5.4 IMAGE RECOGNITION: DEVELOPING A SIMPLE AI VISION SYSTEM

Imagine pointing your phone's camera at a plant, and within seconds, an app identifies it as a Monstera Deliciosa. This magic is made possible by image recognition, a field of artificial intelligence that enables machines to identify and classify objects within images. Whether it's diagnosing medical conditions from X-rays, enhancing security systems with facial recognition, or enabling autonomous vehicles to navigate roads safely, image recognition has a multitude of applications across various sectors.

The first step in developing an image recognition model is selecting and preparing an appropriate dataset. For beginners, datasets like CIFAR-10 or MNIST are ideal. The CIFAR-10 dataset consists of 60,000 32x32 color images in 10 different classes, such as airplanes, cars, and cats. MNIST, on the other hand, contains 70,000 grayscale images of handwritten digits. These datasets are well-suited for learning because they are clean, well-labeled, and relatively small, making them easy to handle.

Start by downloading the dataset and loading it into a data analysis tool like Python's NumPy library. Preprocessing involves:

- Resizing images to a standard size.
- Normalizing pixel values to a range of 0 to 1.
- Augmenting the data by applying transformations like rotations and flips to increase the diversity of the training set.

With your dataset ready, the next step is to build and train the image recognition model. Convolutional Neural Networks (CNNs) are the go-to architecture for image recognition tasks. Begin by defining a simple CNN using a deep learning framework like TensorFlow or PyTorch. A typical CNN architecture consists of convolutional layers that apply filters to the input images, detecting features such as edges and textures. These layers are followed by pooling layers that reduce the spatial dimensions, making the model more computationally efficient. After several convolutional and pooling layers, the data is flattened and passed through fully connected layers, which combine the detected features to make predictions. Once the architecture is defined, compile the model by specifying the loss function and optimizer. Train the model using the training dataset, adjusting parameters like batch size and number of epochs to optimize performance.

Evaluating the model's performance is crucial to ensure it accurately recognizes images. Start by calculating the accuracy, which measures the percentage of correctly classified images. Use a confusion matrix to visualize the model's performance across different classes, identifying areas where it might struggle. For example, if the model frequently confuses cats with dogs, you might need to adjust the training data or fine-tune the model's parameters. Test the model with new, unseen images to assess its generalization capabilities. Finally, deploy the model as a web application using frameworks like Flask. This allows others to interact with your image recognition system through a simple web interface, uploading images and receiving real-time classifications.

Interactive Element: Test Your Image Recognition Model

1. Upload New Images: Gather a set of images that are different from your training dataset.
2. Run Predictions: Use your deployed model to classify these new images.
3. Analyze Results: Compare the model's predictions with the actual labels to assess performance.
4. Improve Model: Based on the analysis, consider further tuning or adding more data to improve accuracy.

Creating an image recognition system offers hands-on experience with AI and provides insight into how machines can learn to see and understand the world. Through this project, you'll gain practical skills in data preprocessing, model building, and deployment, empowering you to explore more advanced AI applications in the future.

5.5 AI IN PERSONAL PROJECTS: BRINGING IDEAS TO LIFE

Imagine sitting at your desk, brainstorming ways to incorporate AI into your daily life. The possibilities are endless, and it all starts with identifying personal project ideas that excite you. Consider home automation using AI, where your smart home devices work seamlessly to create a comfortable living environment. Picture your lights adjusting based on the time of day, your thermostat regulating the temperature to your liking, and your security system recognizing familiar faces. Another intriguing idea could be a personal fitness tracking and recommendation system. This AI-powered tool could analyze your workout data, suggest personalized routines, and even remind you to stay hydrated. Or perhaps you're passionate about managing your finances more effectively. An AI-powered personal finance management app could track your spending habits, offer budgeting tips, and alert you to unusual transactions. The key is choosing a project that aligns with your interests and needs, making the journey enjoyable and rewarding.

Once you've identified a project idea, it's time to move on to the planning and designing phase. Start by defining the project's objectives and scope. Ask yourself what you want to achieve and outline the specific features and functionality your project will include. For example, if you're working on a home automation system, your objectives might be to improve energy efficiency and enhance home security. Next, create a project timeline and set milestones to track your progress. Break the project into manageable tasks, such as researching AI tools, gathering data, and building the model. Designing the system architecture and workflow is also crucial. You'll need to map out how different components will interact and ensure the system is scalable and efficient. Think of this phase as drawing blueprints for a house; a well-thought-out plan will guide the construction process and help you stay organized.

With a solid plan in place, you're ready to implement your project. Choosing suitable AI tools and platforms is the first step. Depending on your project's requirements, you might opt for tools like TensorFlow for building machine learning models or Raspberry Pi for integrating hardware components in home automation. Integrating different components and APIs is the next challenge. For instance, if you're developing a fitness tracking system, you'll need to connect wearable devices to your app and integrate APIs for data collection and analysis. Testing and debugging are essential to ensure your project runs smoothly. Run tests to identify any issues and fix bugs as they arise. It's like troubleshooting a new recipe; adjustments along the way lead to a perfect outcome. Keep refining your project until it meets your expectations, and don't hesitate to seek help from online communities or forums if you encounter challenges.

Once your project is up and running, it's time to showcase and share your work. Creating a project portfolio or blog is an excellent way to document your journey and share your insights with others. Include detailed descriptions, screenshots, and even videos to illustrate how your project works. Sharing code and documentation on platforms like GitHub allows others to learn from your work and contribute to its improvement. Engaging with the AI community through competitions and hackathons can also provide valuable feedback and recognition. These events offer opportunities to present your project, collaborate with like-minded individuals, and gain exposure to new ideas and techniques. By showcasing your project, you demonstrate your skills and inspire others to explore the potential of AI in their personal endeavors.

Engaging in personal AI projects empowers you to bring innovative ideas to life, enhancing your skills and enriching your daily experiences. By identifying a project that resonates with you, meticulously planning and designing it, implementing it with the right tools, and sharing it with the community, you unlock the transformative power of AI in practical and meaningful ways. This chapter has provided a roadmap for embarking on your AI journey, connecting your creativity with technology to create something truly remarkable. In the next chapter, we'll delve into AI's ethical and societal implications, exploring how to navigate the challenges and opportunities that come with this powerful technology.

Interactive Quiz: Hands-On Projects

1. Building Your First AI Model

- **Question**: What is the first step in building a machine learning model?

  a) Writing code without any data
  b) Selecting and preparing a suitable dataset
  c) Testing the model without training it

- **Question**: Which algorithm is recommended for predicting housing prices in this chapter's project?

  a) Decision Tree
  b) K-Nearest Neighbors
  c) Linear Regression

2. Creating a Chatbot

- **Question**: What is the first step in designing a chatbot?

  a) Coding the responses manually
  b) Defining the chatbot's purpose and conversation flow
  c) Deploying the bot without any testing

- **Question**: What are intents and entities in the context of building a chatbot?

a) Intentions and goals of the user without any defined structure
b) Programming terms that mean the same thing
c) Intents are user goals, and entities are pieces of information needed to fulfill those goals

3. Sentiment Analysis with AI

- **Question**: What does sentiment analysis aim to determine?

a) The grammatical correctness of social media posts
b) The emotional tone behind text, identifying whether it's positive, negative, or neutral
c) The popularity of social media accounts

- **Question**: Which algorithms are commonly used for sentiment analysis?

a) Naive Bayes and Support Vector Machine (SVM)
b) K-Means and Linear Regression
c) Random Forest and Decision Tree

4. Image Recognition

- **Question**: Which type of neural network is commonly used for image recognition?

a) Recurrent Neural Network (RNN)
b) Convolutional Neural Network (CNN)

c) Artificial Neural Network (ANN)

- **Question**: What is the purpose of pooling layers in a CNN?

a) To add more features to the model
b) To reduce the spatial dimensions and make the model more efficient
c) To increase the resolution of images

5. AI in Personal Projects

- **Question**: What is the key to choosing a personal AI project?

a) Selecting something random without interest
b) Picking a project that aligns with your interests and needs
c) Choosing the most technically complex idea possible

- **Question**: Why is it important to design a system architecture and workflow before starting implementation?

a) To ensure the project is as difficult as possible
b) To map out how different components interact and maintain organization
c) To skip unnecessary planning and go straight to building

6

ETHICAL AND SOCIETAL IMPLICATION

Imagine you're sitting in a coffee shop, scrolling through your news feed, and you come across a story about a new AI system that's revolutionizing healthcare. It sounds amazing, right? But as you read more, you notice privacy, fairness, and accountability concerns. These issues highlight the importance of ethical AI, ensuring that AI systems are developed, used fairly, and transparent and that human rights are respected. Ethical AI is crucial because it addresses AI technologies' moral and societal implications, ensuring that they benefit everyone without causing harm.

Ethical AI refers to developing and using AI systems in a manner that is fair, transparent, accountable, and respects human rights. Fairness means ensuring AI systems do not perpetuate discrimination or bias. Imagine an AI system used for hiring that unfairly favors one group over another. Such bias can have serious consequences for individuals and society. Transparency involves making AI decision-making processes understandable. When an AI system makes a decision, users should be able to understand how and why that decision was made. Accountability holds developers and users responsible for AI outcomes, ensuring mechanisms are in place to address any harm caused by AI systems. Privacy is about protecting individuals' data and personal information, ensuring that AI systems do not misuse or expose sensitive data.

Leading organizations have developed guidelines and frameworks to promote ethical AI practices. The IEEE Global Initiative on Ethics of Autonomous and Intelligent Systems provides comprehensive guidelines for ethical AI development. These guidelines emphasize the importance of aligning AI systems with human values and promoting well-being. The European Union's Ethics Guidelines for Trustworthy AI outline key requirements for AI systems, including accountability, transparency, and fairness. These guidelines ensure that AI systems are trustworthy and respect fundamental rights. The Asilomar AI Principles, developed by a group of AI researchers and thought leaders, provide a set of principles to guide the development and use of AI. These principles emphasize the importance of safety, transparency, and ethical considerations in AI research and development.

Implementing ethical AI practices requires practical steps that can be integrated into AI development and usage. Conducting ethical impact assessments is a crucial step. These assessments evaluate AI systems' potential ethical and societal impacts, identifying risks and ensuring that measures are in place to mitigate them. Establishing ethics review boards can provide oversight and guidance, ensuring that AI projects align with ethical standards. Engaging with diverse stakeholders, including ethicists, policymakers, and community representatives, ensures that multiple perspectives are considered in AI development. This engagement fosters a collaborative approach to ethical AI, promoting inclusivity and fairness. Continuous monitoring and evaluation mechanisms are essential to ensure that AI systems remain aligned with ethical principles throughout their lifecycle. This includes regular audits, updates, and feedback loops to address any emerging ethical concerns.

Interactive Element: Ethical AI Checklist

Checklist for Developing Ethical AI:

1. Fairness:

- Ensure datasets are diverse and representative.
- Implement measures to detect and mitigate bias.
- Regularly review and update algorithms to maintain fairness.

2. Transparency:

- Make AI decision-making processes understandable to users.
- Provide clear explanations for AI decisions and outcomes.
- Publish documentation and reports on AI system operations.

3. Accountability:

- Establish clear lines of responsibility for AI outcomes.
- Implement mechanisms for addressing harm caused by AI systems.
- Ensure accountability through oversight and governance structures.

4. Privacy:

- Protect individuals' data through encryption and anonymization.
- Obtain informed consent for data collection and usage.
- Regularly audit data usage and compliance with privacy regulations.

Following this checklist ensures that your AI projects align with ethical principles, promoting fairness, transparency, accountability, and privacy.

6.1 PRIVACY CONCERNS: SAFEGUARDING PERSONAL DATA IN AI SYSTEMS

Imagine using a health app that tracks your daily activity, sleep patterns, and heart rate. This app collects vast amounts of data about you, storing it to provide personalized health insights. While the benefits are clear, the potential privacy risks are significant. AI systems often require large datasets to function effectively, raising concerns about how this data is collected, stored, and used. The more data these systems gather, the greater the risk of misuse or unauthorized access. If not properly safeguarded, personal information can be exposed, leading to privacy breaches that impact your life in ways you might not have anticipated. Protecting this data becomes paramount to ensure that your personal information remains secure.

To address these concerns, various regulations have been established globally to govern the use of personal data in AI systems. The General Data Protection Regulation (GDPR) in the European Union sets strict guidelines on data protection and privacy. It mandates that organizations obtain explicit consent from individuals before collecting their data and ensure that this data is securely stored and processed. Similarly, the California Consumer Privacy Act (CCPA) in the United States gives residents the right to know what personal data is being collected and how it is used. It also allows them to request the deletion of their data. In Singapore, the Personal Data Protection Act (PDPA) regulates personal data collection, use, and disclosure, ensuring that organizations handle data responsibly. These regulations protect individuals' privacy rights and hold organizations accountable for data misuse.

Implementing best practices for data privacy in AI systems is crucial to safeguarding personal information. Data anonymization and encryption techniques are fundamental. Anonymization involves removing personally identifiable information from datasets, making it impossible to trace the data back to individuals. Encryption ensures that data is converted into a secure format that can only be accessed by authorized users. Robust access controls are also essential, restricting data access to only those who need it for legitimate purposes. Regularly auditing data usage and compliance helps identify any lapses in security and ensures that data handling practices align with regulatory standards. Obtaining informed consent from data subjects is another critical step. This means clearly explaining how their data will be used and giving them the choice to opt in or out. Organizations can build trust and protect personal data by implementing these measures.

Real-world examples of privacy breaches involving AI highlight the consequences of inadequate data protection. The Cambridge Analytica and Facebook data scandal is a notable case. Personal data from millions of Facebook users was harvested without consent and used for political advertising, leading to widespread outrage and legal repercussions. Another example involves health data breaches, where AI-powered diagnostic tools exposed sensitive patient information. These incidents underscore the importance of robust data protection measures. When personal data is mishandled, the impact can be far-reaching, affecting individuals' privacy, security, and trust in technology. These breaches serve as a reminder of the need for stringent data protection practices in AI systems.

Case Study: Cambridge Analytica and Facebook Data Scandal

Scenario: In 2018, it was revealed that Cambridge Analytica had harvested data from millions of Facebook profiles without user consent to influence political campaigns.

Key Points:

1. Data Collection: Personal data was collected through a quiz app, which accessed not just the quiz takers' information but also their friends' data.

2. Usage: The data was used to create detailed voter profiles and target political ads, significantly impacting the 2016 US presidential election.
3. Consequences: The scandal led to legal actions, regulatory changes, and a loss of user trust in Facebook.

Reflection:

1. What measures could have prevented the unauthorized data collection?
2. How can organizations ensure transparency in data usage to maintain user trust?

Understanding privacy concerns in AI systems and implementing best practices for data protection are crucial steps in safeguarding personal information. By adhering to regulations and learning from past breaches, we can build a future where AI technologies enhance our lives without compromising our privacy.

6.2 AI AND JOB DISPLACEMENT: PREPARING FOR THE FUTURE OF WORK

Imagine waking up one day to find that your job has been automated. AI and automation are transforming the job market, making some roles obsolete while creating new opportunities in AI-related fields. For instance, robots now perform repetitive manufacturing tasks with remarkable precision. This shift means fewer assembly line workers but an increased demand for engineers who can design, maintain, and program these robots. Similarly, automated checkout systems in retail reduce the need for cashiers but create roles in tech support and system management.

Industries such as manufacturing and production are experiencing significant changes due to AI. Automated systems can assemble products faster and more accurately than humans, leading to increased efficiency and job losses for manual laborers. Retail and customer service sectors are also affected. Chatbots handle customer inquiries 24/7, reducing the need for human operators. Autonomous vehicles are beginning to replace traditional drivers in ride-sharing services and logistics. Healthcare is not immune to these changes either. AI diagnostic tools and robotic surgeries are transforming how medical services are delivered, impacting jobs for medical technicians and administrative staff.

To navigate this changing landscape, individuals and organizations need to adopt strategies for workforce adaptation. Reskilling and upskilling programs are vital. These initiatives help workers acquire new skills that are in demand, such as data analysis or machine learning. Lifelong learning initiatives encourage continuous education, ensuring workers remain relevant in their fields. Government and corporate policies can support workforce transitions by funding training programs and incentives for businesses to reskill their employees. Fostering a culture of innovation and adaptability within organizations helps employees embrace new technologies and view change as an opportunity rather than a threat.

Consider the case of a traditional manufacturing company that successfully adapted to AI-driven changes. The company implemented a comprehensive reskilling program, training its assembly line workers to operate and maintain new robotic systems. This transition not only preserved jobs but also improved productivity and worker satisfaction. Another example is an individual transitioning from a customer service role to a tech support position. By enrolling in online courses and earning certifications in AI and data science, they were able to leverage their customer service experience while embracing new opportunities in the tech industry.

Reskilling and upskilling programs have shown remarkable success in these transitions. Companies that invest in their employees' education retain valuable talent and foster a more innovative and adaptable workforce. For instance, a logistics firm introduced AI-driven route optimization software. Rather than laying off drivers, the company provided training on using the new technology. This approach improved operational efficiency and empowered drivers, giving them new skills that enhanced their job security.

Individuals can also take proactive steps to prepare for the future of work. Engaging in lifelong learning initiatives, such as enrolling in online courses or attending workshops, keeps skills up-to-date. Networking with professionals in emerging fields and staying informed about industry trends can provide insights into new career opportunities. By embracing a mindset of continuous learning and adaptability, individuals can confidently navigate the changing job landscape.

In healthcare, AI diagnostic tools have significantly improved the accuracy and speed of medical diagnoses. However, this has also impacted jobs for medical technicians who traditionally perform these tasks. To adapt, many healthcare professionals undergo training in AI and data analytics, enabling them to work alongside AI systems and enhance patient care. Integrating human expertise with AI technology is transforming healthcare delivery, making it more efficient and effective.

Fostering a culture of innovation and adaptability within organizations is crucial. Encouraging employees to experiment with new technologies, providing opportunities for continuous learning, and recognizing the value of diverse skill sets can drive organizational success in the AI era. By creating an environment that supports innovation, businesses can thrive amidst technological advancements and ensure their workforce remains resilient and capable of meeting new challenges.

6.3 BIAS IN AI: IDENTIFYING AND MITIGATING RISKS

Imagine you're using an AI-powered hiring tool to select candidates for a job. You notice that the system seems to favor certain demographics over others. This is an example of bias in AI, a systematic error that results in unfair outcomes. Bias in AI often stems from biased training data or flawed algorithms. When an AI model is trained on data that reflects societal prejudices, it can perpetuate those biases, leading to discriminatory decisions. For instance, if historical hiring data shows a preference for a particular gender or ethnicity, the AI system may learn to replicate that bias, disadvantaging other groups.

Various types of bias can affect AI systems. Data bias occurs when the training data is unrepresentative or skewed. For example, if a facial recognition system is trained primarily on images of light-skinned individuals, it may perform poorly on darker-skinned faces. Algorithmic bias results from the design or implementation of algorithms. This can happen when certain features are weighted more heavily than others, skewing the results. Selection bias arises from non-random sampling of data. If the data collected for training an AI model does not accurately represent the population, the model's predictions will be biased. Each type of bias can significantly impact the fairness and accuracy of AI systems.

Identifying bias in AI systems requires systematic techniques. Conducting bias audits and fairness tests is a crucial step. These audits involve evaluating the AI system to detect any discriminatory patterns or outcomes. Analyzing decision-making patterns can reveal inconsistencies and biases in the model's predictions. For instance, if an AI hiring tool disproportionately rejects candidates from a particular demographic, this pattern must be addressed. Using fairness metrics like disparate impact and equal opportunity helps quantify bias. Disparate impact measures whether the AI system's decisions disproportionately affect certain groups, while equal opportunity ensures that all groups have a fair chance of positive outcomes.

Mitigating bias in AI systems involves several strategies. Ensuring diverse and representative training data is paramount. This means collecting data from a wide range of sources to reflect the diversity of the population. Implementing algorithmic fairness techniques can help balance the model's decisions. For example, re-weighting certain features or using fairness constraints can reduce bias. Involving diverse teams in AI development is also crucial. When people from different backgrounds contribute to designing and implementing AI systems, they bring varied perspectives that can help identify and mitigate biases. Regularly monitoring and updating AI systems is essential to address emerging biases. As societal norms and data evolve, continuous evaluation ensures that AI systems remain fair and unbiased.

Interactive Element: Bias Detection Exercise

Exercise: Identifying Bias in an AI System:

1. Collect Data: Gather a dataset used by an AI system, such as hiring data or loan applications.
2. Analyze Patterns: Examine the decisions made by the AI system, looking for patterns that indicate bias (e.g., higher rejection rates for certain groups).

3. Conduct Fairness Tests: Use fairness metrics like disparate impact to quantify bias. Compare the outcomes for different demographic groups.
4. Evaluate Results: Determine whether the AI system's decisions are fair and unbiased. Identify areas where bias is present and needs to be addressed.

By understanding and addressing the different types of bias in AI systems, you can ensure that these technologies are fair and equitable. Identifying bias through systematic techniques and implementing strategies to mitigate it promotes fairness in AI applications. This approach fosters trust in AI systems and ensures that they benefit everyone, regardless of their background.

6.4 AI GOVERNANCE: POLICIES AND REGULATIONS AROUND THE WORLD

Imagine you're a developer working on a new AI application that has the potential to revolutionize healthcare. But before you can deploy your innovation, you must navigate numerous policies and regulations. AI governance is crucial for ensuring that AI technologies are developed and used responsibly. It involves establishing policies, regulations, and frameworks that guide AI's ethical and responsible use. This governance is essential to prevent misuse, protect individuals, and promote trust in AI technologies. Without these guidelines, the rapid advancement of AI could lead to unintended consequences, including ethical breaches and privacy violations.

Around the world, different countries and regions have implemented various AI policies and regulations to address these concerns. The European Union's AI Act is a comprehensive regulatory framework to ensure AI systems are safe and respect fundamental rights. It categorizes AI systems based on their risk levels and imposes strict requirements on high-risk applications. In the United States, AI governance is shaped by federal and state initiatives, including executive orders promoting AI innovation while addressing ethical and safety concerns. China's AI development plan outlines its strategy to become a global leader in AI by 2030, emphasizing both technological advancement and regulatory oversight. Singapore's Model AI Governance Framework provides practical guidance for organizations to implement ethical AI practices, focusing on transparency, accountability, and human-centric design.

Effective AI governance frameworks share several key components that ensure their robustness and applicability. Ethical guidelines and principles form the foundation, outlining the values and standards that AI systems must adhere to. These guidelines ensure that AI technologies align with societal norms and ethical considerations. Regulatory oversight and enforcement mechanisms are crucial for monitoring compliance and addressing violations. This oversight includes regular audits, inspections, and penalties for non-compliance. Stakeholder engagement and collaboration are essential to incorporate diverse perspectives and expertise in AI governance. This engagement fosters a collaborative approach, ensuring that the interests of various stakeholders, including the public, are considered. Transparency and accountability measures are vital for building trust in AI systems. These measures require organizations to disclose how their AI systems work and to be accountable for their outcomes, enabling users to understand and trust the technology.

However, implementing AI governance has its challenges. One significant challenge is balancing innovation with regulation. Overly stringent regulations can stifle innovation, while lax regulations can lead to ethical breaches and misuse. Finding the right balance requires continuous dialogue between regulators, developers, and stakeholders. Addressing cross-border data flows and jurisdictional issues is another challenge. As AI systems often operate globally, differences in regulations across countries can complicate compliance. Harmonizing these regulations and fostering international cooperation are essential for effective governance. Adapting to rapid technological advancements is also a significant challenge. AI technologies evolve quickly, and governance frameworks must be flexible and adaptable to keep pace with these changes. This adaptability ensures that regulations remain relevant and effective in addressing new ethical and safety concerns.

The future of AI governance involves fostering international cooperation to address these challenges. Collaborative efforts between countries, organizations, and stakeholders can lead to the development of unified standards and best practices. These standards promote consistency and fairness in AI governance, ensuring that AI technologies benefit everyone. As AI continues to evolve, governance frameworks must also evolve, incorporating new insights, technologies, and ethical considerations. By fostering a culture of continuous improvement and collaboration, we can ensure that AI technologies are developed and used responsibly, benefiting society as a whole.

In this chapter, we've explored the critical aspects of ethical and societal implications of AI, from ethical principles and data privacy to job displacement and governance. Understanding these facets is essential for navigating the complex landscape of AI responsibly. As we move forward, we'll delve into the future trends and innovations in AI, exploring what lies ahead in this rapidly evolving field.

Interactive Quiz: Ethical and Societal Implications

1. Understanding Ethical AI

- **Question**: What does ethical AI aim to ensure?

  a) AI systems are developed and used fairly, transparently, and accountably
  b) AI focuses only on maximizing profits
  c) AI systems operate without any oversight or regulations

- **Question**: Which of the following is a key principle of ethical AI?

  a) Speed of development
  b) Transparency and explainability
  c) Reducing system updates

2. Privacy Concerns in AI

- **Question**: What is a primary concern regarding personal data in AI systems?

  a) Reducing the amount of data collected
  b) The misuse or unauthorized access to sensitive information
  c) Ensuring data remains completely unprocessed

- **Question**: Which regulation focuses on data protection and privacy in the European Union?

  a) California Consumer Privacy Act (CCPA)
  b) General Data Protection Regulation (GDPR)

c) Personal Data Protection Act (PDPA)

3. AI and Job Displacement

- **Question**: How can individuals prepare for the impact of AI on the job market?

a) Avoiding any form of skill development
b) Engaging in reskilling and upskilling programs
c) Relying solely on outdated methods

- **Question**: What is a key strategy for organizations to adapt to AI-driven changes in the workforce?

  a) Encouraging resistance to new technologies
  b) Fostering a culture of innovation and adaptability
  c) Reducing learning opportunities for employees

4. Bias in AI

- **Question**: What is a common cause of bias in AI systems?

  a) Randomized data collection
  b) Biased training data that reflects societal prejudices
  c) Testing the model only with diverse data

- **Question**: Which strategy is recommended for mitigating bias in AI systems?

  a) Using limited, non-representative datasets
  b) Ensuring diverse and representative training data
  c) Ignoring fairness metrics during model evaluation

5. AI Governance

- **Question**: What is the purpose of AI governance?

  a) To establish policies and regulations that guide responsible AI development and use
  b) To increase the speed of AI development without ethical considerations
  c) To allow unrestricted deployment of AI technologies

- **Question**: What is a challenge in implementing AI governance?

  a) Balancing innovation with regulation
  b) Avoiding the development of new technologies
  c) Limiting the number of stakeholders involved in decision-making

7

FUTURE TRENDS IN AI

I magine you're sipping your morning coffee, scrolling through the latest tech news, when you come across an article about quantum computing. The headline promises a future where computers can solve problems in seconds, taking today's fastest supercomputers thousands of years. This isn't a sci-fi dream but a rapidly approaching reality. Quantum computing is poised to revolutionize AI, unlocking possibilities we can only begin to imagine.

7.1 QUANTUM COMPUTING AND AI: A REVOLUTIONARY COMBINATION

Quantum computing is a new paradigm in computing that leverages the principles of quantum mechanics. Unlike classical computers that use bits as the smallest unit of data, quantum computers use quantum bits or qubits. What makes qubits fascinating is their ability to exist in multiple states simultaneously, thanks to a property called superposition. This means a qubit can represent both 0 and 1 at the same time. Additionally, qubits can be entangled, a phenomenon where the state of one qubit is directly related to the state of another, no matter the distance between them. These properties enable quantum computers to perform massively parallel processing, making them exponentially more powerful than classical computers for certain tasks.

The potential impact of quantum computing on AI is nothing short of transformative. One of the most significant advantages is the ability to solve complex optimization problems much faster than classical computers. For instance, current AI algorithms often require extensive time and resources to find the optimal solution in tasks like route planning or resource allocation. Quantum computing could reduce this time from years to mere seconds. Machine learning, a subset of AI, stands to benefit immensely. Model training times could be drastically shortened, allowing quicker iterations and improvements. This acceleration would enable AI systems to learn from larger datasets, leading to more accurate predictions and better performance. Moreover, quantum computing could enhance simulations and predictions, providing more detailed and precise models of complex systems, from climate models to financial markets.

Ongoing research and development in quantum computing are already yielding promising results. In 2019, Google announced that its quantum computer, Sycamore, had achieved quantum supremacy. This means it performed a calculation in 200 seconds that would take the fastest classical supercomputer approximately 10,000 years. IBM is also making significant strides with its quantum computing initiatives, offering cloud-based access to quantum processors for researchers and developers worldwide. Microsoft's Quantum Development Kit provides tools to create quantum algorithms, making it easier for developers to experiment with this cutting-edge technology. These advancements highlight the rapid progress in the field and the growing interest in integrating quantum computing with AI.

However, the road to fully integrating quantum computing with AI is challenging. One of the primary obstacles is qubit stability. Qubits are highly sensitive to their environment, and even minor disturbances can cause errors, a problem known as decoherence. Researchers are working on error-correcting codes and more stable qubit designs to mitigate this issue. Another challenge is developing quantum algorithms tailored for AI applications. While classical algorithms have been refined over decades, quantum algorithms are still in their infancy. Significant research is needed to create algorithms that can leverage quantum computing's unique capabilities. Additionally, building scalable quantum computing infrastructure is a monumental task. Current quantum computers still need to improve in terms of the number of qubits they can handle. Scaling these systems to support millions of qubits will require engineering and materials science breakthroughs. Despite these challenges, the potential rewards make the pursuit worthwhile. Experts predict practical quantum-AI applications could become a reality within the next decade, ushering in unprecedented computational power and innovation.

Explore Further: Quantum Computing Resources

1. Quantum Computing for the Very Curious by Michael Nielsen: A comprehensive online book that explains quantum computing in an accessible way.
2. IBM Quantum Experience: Access IBM's quantum computers through the cloud and experiment with quantum algorithms.
3. Microsoft Quantum Development Kit: Download tools and resources to start building quantum algorithms.

As you delve deeper into AI and quantum computing, keep an eye on these developments. The fusion of these two groundbreaking fields promises a future where the limits of what we can achieve are redefined, opening doors to innovations that will shape the world for future generations.

7.2 AI IN SPACE EXPLORATION: BEYOND EARTHLY APPLICATIONS

Picture this: a spacecraft navigating the vast expanse of space, autonomously adjusting its course to avoid a potential collision with space debris. This isn't the plot of a sci-fi movie but a current application of AI in space missions. AI plays a crucial role in autonomous spacecraft navigation, enabling these vehicles to make real-time decisions based on data from sensors and cameras. This capability is vital for missions where human intervention is limited or delayed due to the vast distances involved. Moreover, AI helps analyze vast amounts of data collected by space telescopes, identifying patterns and anomalies that might take human researchers years to process. For instance, AI algorithms sift through data from the Hubble Space Telescope, discovering new celestial bodies and phenomena. Another critical application is predicting and mitigating space weather effects. AI models analyze solar activity and predict solar flares, which can disrupt Earth's satellite communications and power grids.

AI-driven robots and rovers have become indispensable tools in space exploration. NASA's Mars rovers, such as Curiosity and Perseverance, use AI for autonomous operations. These rovers navigate the Martian terrain, analyze soil and rock samples, and send valuable data back to Earth, all with minimal human inter-vention. AI enables these rovers to make decisions on the fly, selecting the most promising sites for exploration and avoiding potential hazards. Robotic arms equipped with AI handle delicate tasks such as satellite repairs and assembly in space. These robots can perform precise maneuvers, reducing the risk to human astro-nauts and increasing the efficiency of space missions. AI is also pivotal in lunar and asteroid exploration missions. For example, Japan's Hayabusa2 mission used AI to land on an asteroid, collect samples, and return them to Earth, providing invaluable insights into the early solar system.

Astronauts benefit from AI assistance in various aspects of space missions. AI-powered virtual assistants help astronauts with mission planning and troubleshooting. These assistants provide real-time information, answer questions, and offer solutions to technical problems, making daily operations smoother and more efficient. Health monitoring systems using AI track astronauts' well-being, analyzing vital signs and detecting early signs of health issues. These systems can predict potential health problems and suggest preventive measures, ensuring astronauts remain in optimal condition. AI also plays a role in managing life support systems. It monitors and adjusts oxygen levels, carbon dioxide, and other vital parameters, ensuring a safe and habitable environment for astronauts during long-duration missions.

The future of AI in space exploration holds exciting prospects. The Artemis program, aiming to return humans to the Moon and establish a sustainable presence, will leverage AI technologies for exploration and habitat management. AI systems will assist in navigating the lunar surface, identifying resources, and supporting construction activities. The James Webb Space Telescope, set to launch soon, will use AI for advanced data analysis, helping scientists uncover the mysteries of the universe. Planned missions to Mars and beyond will also rely heavily on AI. These missions will involve complex tasks such as autonomous navigation, resource utilization, and habitat construction, all of which will benefit from the capabilities of AI. As we continue to push the boundaries of space exploration, AI will undoubtedly play a central role in overcoming the challenges and seizing the opportunities that lie ahead.

7.3 THE EVOLUTION OF AI: FUTURE TECHNOLOGIES AND INNOVATIONS

Imagine you're exploring a bustling city, and every corner you turn, there's a smart device guiding your way. This is the future landscape where emerging AI technologies will play a pivotal role. One of the most exciting developments is Explainable AI (XAI). Unlike traditional AI models, which often operate as "black boxes," XAI aims to make AI decisions transparent and understandable. This involves developing systems that can explain their reasoning in human terms, ensuring users understand why a particular decision was made. Imagine an AI in healthcare that not only diagnoses a condition but also explains the basis of its diagnosis.

Another groundbreaking area is AI-driven edge computing. Traditional AI systems often rely on centralized data centers to process information, but edge computing brings AI closer to data sources like sensors and devices. This shift enables real-time processing and decision-making, which is crucial for applications like autonomous vehicles and smart cities. For instance, imagine a traffic light system that uses edge computing to manage traffic flow dynamically, reducing congestion and improving safety in real time.

Neuromorphic computing is another frontier in AI technology. Inspired by the human brain's architecture, neuromorphic chips aim to mimic neural networks' efficiency and speed. These chips can process information faster and more efficiently than traditional processors, opening new possibilities for AI applications. Picture a wearable health monitor that uses neuromorphic chips to continuously analyze vital signs and provide instant feedback, potentially saving lives by predicting health issues before they become critical.

Advancements in AI hardware are driving the next generation of AI systems. AI-specific processors like Google's Tensor Processing Units (TPUs) and NVIDIA's Graphics Processing Units (GPUs) are designed to handle the massive computational demands of AI tasks. These processors accelerate deep learning models, making them faster and more efficient. Imagine training a complex neural network in hours instead of days, enabling quicker iterations and innovations. Innovations in photonic computing are also on the horizon. By using light instead of electrical signals, photonic chips promise to perform computations at the speed of light, vastly improving processing speeds and energy efficiency.

AI is making inroads into emerging fields, opening novel possibilities. In genomics and personalized medicine, AI analyzes vast amounts of genetic data to identify patterns and predict disease risks. This leads to personalized treatment plans tailored to an individual's genetic makeup. Imagine a future where your doctor uses AI to craft a treatment plan specifically for you, maximizing effectiveness and minimizing side effects. Environmental monitoring is another area where AI shines. AI models analyze data from sensors and satellites to monitor environmental changes and predict natural disasters. This can help mitigate the impacts of climate change and protect vulnerable communities. AI optimizes urban infrastructure in smart cities, from managing energy consumption to coordinating public transportation. Picture a city where AI ensures efficient energy use, reduces pollution, and enhances the quality of life for its residents.

Future research directions are set to drive further AI innovations. Advances in unsupervised and self-supervised learning are particularly promising. These techniques allow AI systems to learn from unlabeled data, making them more adaptable and efficient. Research in AI-human collaboration and co-learning is also gaining traction. This involves developing AI systems that can work alongside humans, enhancing our capabilities and fostering a symbiotic relationship. Imagine a workplace where AI assists you in tasks, freeing you to focus on creative and strategic activities. Developments in transfer learning and meta-learning are also exciting. These approaches enable AI systems to apply knowledge from one domain to another, accelerating learning and adaptation. Explorations in artificial general intelligence (AGI) aim to create AI systems with human-like cognitive abilities that are capable of understanding, learning, and applying knowledge across a wide range of tasks.

7.4 AI AND HUMAN INTERACTION: THE NEXT FRONTIER

Imagine sitting in your living room, asking your smart speaker to play your favorite song, and it instantly responds. This isn't just a convenience; it's a glimpse into how AI enhances human-computer interaction. Natural language processing (NLP) powers these voice-activated assistants, allowing them to understand and respond to spoken commands. This technology makes interacting with devices more intuitive and accessible, breaking down barriers for those who might not be tech-savvy. Beyond voice commands, AI-driven gesture recognition systems add another layer of inter-action. For example, you can wave your hand to navigate through a presentation or use finger movements to control a virtual envi-ronment. Emotion recognition in AI also makes strides, enabling systems to gauge your mood through facial expressions or voice tone and offer personalized interactions, such as adjusting lighting or music to suit your emotional state.

In augmented and virtual reality (AR/VR), AI pushes the bound-aries of immersive experiences. Imagine putting on a VR headset and finding yourself in a lifelike simulation for training or educa-tion. AI enhances these virtual environments by creating realistic scenarios and characters that respond dynamically to your actions. For instance, in a medical training simulation, AI can generate virtual patients exhibiting various symptoms, allowing medical students to practice diagnosing and treating different conditions. Augmented reality applications use AI for real-time object recog-nition, superimposing useful information onto the physical world. Imagine walking through a museum and pointing your smart-phone at an exhibit to receive detailed information about it instantly. AI also helps create realistic virtual characters and environments, making games and simulations more engaging and lifelike.

Assistive technologies for individuals with disabilities are another area where AI shines. AI-powered speech-to-text systems convert spoken words into written text, aiding those with hearing impairments in communication. Conversely, text-to-speech systems help visually impaired individuals with difficulty speaking. Imagine a visually impaired person using a smartphone app to read aloud messages and emails. AI is also instrumental in developing smart prosthetics and exoskeletons. These devices use AI to interpret signals from the user's body, allowing for more natural movements and improving mobility. For instance, an AI-driven prosthetic hand can learn and adapt to the user's muscle signals, offering better control and functionality. Navigation aids for visually impaired individuals powered by AI can analyze their surroundings and provide real-time guidance, making navigating complex environments easier.

However, integrating AI into human interaction brings ethical considerations that must be considered. Privacy is a significant concern, especially with AI systems that collect and analyze personal data. Ensuring AI's ethical design and use in personal assistants is crucial to protect user privacy. Imagine an AI assistant that listens to your conversations to improve its responses. While this can enhance functionality, it raises questions about data security and consent. Addressing privacy concerns in AI-driven surveillance systems is equally important. These systems can enhance security but must be designed to prevent misuse and protect individuals' rights. Trust is another critical factor in AI-human collaboration. Fostering trust requires transparency in how AI systems operate and make decisions. Users need to understand and trust the AI systems they interact with, whether virtual assistants, medical diagnosis tools, or security systems.

As AI continues to evolve, its role in enhancing human interaction will only grow. The potential to make technology more intuitive, inclusive, and responsive is immense. AI transforms how we interact with the world, from voice-activated assistants and gesture recognition systems to immersive AR/VR experiences and assistive technologies. However, navigating the ethical landscape is essential to ensure these advancements benefit everyone while protecting their rights and privacy.

7.5 PREDICTING AI TRENDS: WHAT'S NEXT IN THE AI WORLD?

AI is expected to continue profoundly transforming the workplace and the job market in the coming years. Imagine a future where mundane, repetitive tasks are fully automated, freeing up human workers to engage in more creative and strategic activities. AI is already making strides in this direction, automating routine tasks such as data entry, scheduling, and even customer service interactions. This shift allows employees to focus on tasks that require human ingenuity and emotional intelligence. As AI continues to evolve, new job roles, such as AI ethicists, data curators, and machine learning specialists, will create opportunities for those willing to adapt and learn new skills. Lifelong learning will become a cornerstone of career development. With AI's rapid advancements, staying current with the latest technologies and continuously updating one's skillset will be crucial for career growth and job security. This dynamic landscape will demand a flexible and adaptable workforce.

AI's potential to address global challenges is another exciting frontier. In the fight against climate change, AI can analyze vast datasets to create accurate climate models, predict natural disasters, and optimize renewable energy sources. Imagine an AI system that monitors global weather patterns in real-time, predicting hurricanes and wildfires with unprecedented accuracy, allowing for timely evacuations and disaster response. AI can revolutionize patient care by predicting disease outbreaks, personalizing treatments, and improving diagnostics in healthcare. For example, AI-driven models can identify patterns in medical data to predict the spread of infectious diseases, enabling public health officials to implement preventive measures swiftly. AI offers personalized learning experiences in education, adapting to each student's needs and pace, making education more accessible and effective. Picture a classroom where AI tutors provide real-time feedback, helping students grasp complex concepts and stay engaged.

The evolving landscape of AI governance and policy is crucial for ensuring AI technologies' responsible development and deployment. International cooperation and collaborative AI governance initiatives are essential for creating a cohesive framework that addresses ethical and privacy concerns. For instance, countries worldwide are working together to establish guidelines and standards for AI ethics, ensuring that AI systems are fair, transparent, and accountable. Evolving AI ethics and data privacy regulations are being implemented to protect individuals' rights and foster trust in AI. These regulations impact innovation and competitiveness, as companies must balance compliance with the need to stay at the forefront of technological advancements. Policymakers are also exploring ways to promote inclusive AI development, ensuring that the benefits of AI are shared equitably across society.

Public perception of AI and its broader societal impact is another critical aspect to consider. As AI becomes more integrated into daily life, educating the public on AI's benefits and risks is essential. Public awareness campaigns and educational programs can help demystify AI, addressing fears and misconceptions. For instance, many people worry that AI will lead to widespread job loss. Still, these concerns can be alleviated by highlighting how AI can augment human capabilities and create new job opportunities. Promoting inclusive and equitable AI development is also vital. Ensuring that AI technologies are designed and deployed with diversity and inclusivity in mind can help mitigate biases and create more fair and just systems. By fostering a better understanding of AI and its potential, we can build a society that embraces technological advancements while addressing the ethical and societal challenges they bring.

As we explore these future trends, it's clear that AI's potential to transform various aspects of our lives is immense. The workplace will evolve, offering new opportunities and demanding continuous learning. AI will be pivotal in addressing global challenges, from climate change to healthcare and education. Effective governance and policy frameworks will guide the responsible development of AI, while public perception and societal impact will shape its integration into daily life. Understanding and embracing these trends will be key to unlocking AI's full potential as we navigate this exciting landscape.

Interactive Quiz: Future Trends in AI

1. Quantum Computing and AI

- **Question**: What makes quantum computing different from classical computing?

  a) Quantum computers use regular bits for data processing.
  b) Quantum computers use qubits, which can exist in multiple states simultaneously.

c) Quantum computing has slower processing speeds than classical computing.

- **Question**: Which of the following is a major benefit of quantum computing for AI?

a) Slower data processing
b) Drastically shorter model training times
c) Inability to handle large datasets

2. AI in Space Exploration

- **Question**: How is AI used in autonomous spacecraft navigation?

a) AI enables spacecraft to make real-time decisions without human intervention.
b) AI slows down data analysis for space missions.
c) AI is not used in space exploration.

- **Question**: What role does AI play in assisting astronauts during space missions?

a) AI only performs non-critical tasks.
b) AI-powered virtual assistants help with mission planning and troubleshooting.
c) AI systems are not involved in space missions.

3. The Evolution of AI

- **Question**: What is Explainable AI (XAI)?

  a) AI systems that operate as "black boxes."
  b) AI systems that provide understandable explanations for their decisions.
  c) AI that is exclusively used in gaming.

- **Question**: What is edge computing in the context of AI?

  a) Centralizing all AI processing in data centers
  b) Bringing AI processing closer to data sources for real-time decision-making
  c) A way to slow down AI responses

4. AI and Human Interaction

- **Question**: How does AI enhance human-computer interaction?

  a) By making interfaces less user-friendly
  b) Through natural language processing, gesture recognition, and emotion detection
  c) By removing voice-activated systems

- **Question**: Which of the following is a key ethical concern in AI-enhanced human interaction?

  a) Lack of processing power
  b) Privacy and data security issues
  c) The inability to automate tasks

5. Predicting AI Trends

- **Question**: How is AI expected to transform the future workplace?

  a) By automating all jobs and eliminating human involvement
  b) By automating repetitive tasks and creating opportunities for more creative work
  c) By slowing down workplace efficiency

- **Question**: Why is international cooperation important for AI governance?

  a) To limit AI research to one country
  b) To establish consistent ethical standards and regulations globally
  c) To reduce the development of AI technologies

8

CAREER PROSPECTS IN AI

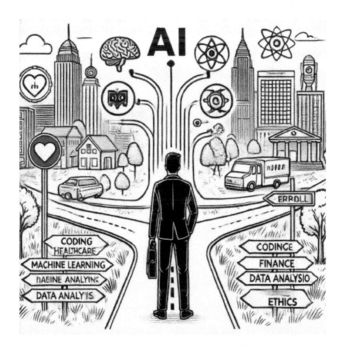

I magine walking into a bustling job fair, where the energy is palpable, and the possibilities seem endless. You hear snippets of conversations about machine learning, neural networks, and AI ethics. Recruiters from top tech firms, healthcare giants, and financial institutions eagerly discuss the transformative power of AI, offering enticing roles to those with the right skills. This scene captures the essence of the current job market, where AI professionals are in high demand across various sectors. The opportunities are vast, and the need for skilled individuals is growing exponentially, making this an exciting time to dive into a career in AI.

8.1 AI IN THE JOB MARKET: SKILLS IN DEMAND

The demand for AI talent is skyrocketing across multiple industries. Tech companies, in particular, are always looking for AI experts who can help develop innovative products and services. Giants like Google, Amazon, and Microsoft are investing heavily in AI research and development, creating many job opportunities. But the tech sector is just the tip of the iceberg. The healthcare industry increasingly relies on AI for everything from diagnostics to personalized treatment plans. Financial institutions employ AI to enhance fraud detection, risk management, and customer service. Retail is tapping into AI to improve inventory management and create personalized shopping experiences. Emerging roles in AI ethics and governance are also gaining traction as organizations recognize the importance of ethical AI practices.

To thrive in this competitive job market, you need a robust set of technical skills. Proficiency in machine learning frameworks like TensorFlow and PyTorch is highly sought after. These frameworks enable you to build and deploy machine learning models efficiently. Experience with data analysis and visualization tools, such as Pandas, Matplotlib, and Tableau, is equally important. These tools help you understand large datasets and present your findings. Knowledge of programming languages like Python and R is almost a prerequisite, as they are the backbone of most AI projects. Understanding neural network architectures and deep learning techniques is crucial, especially if you aim to work on complex projects involving image recognition, natural language processing, or autonomous systems.

However, technical expertise alone is not enough. Employers also value soft skills that complement your technical abilities. Problem-solving and critical thinking are essential, as AI projects often involve tackling complex challenges and finding innovative solutions. Strong communication and teamwork skills are crucial, as you'll frequently collaborate with cross-functional teams. An adaptability and continuous learning mindset will help you stay current with the rapidly evolving AI landscape. Ethical decision-making and responsibility are increasingly important, particularly as AI systems impact more aspects of our daily lives. Navigating ethical dilemmas and ensuring fair use of AI technologies can set you apart in the job market.

Different industries also require specialized skills tailored to their unique needs. For instance, knowledge of medical imaging and health informatics is invaluable in healthcare. AI professionals in this field must understand how to analyze medical images and work with electronic health records. In finance, understanding financial modeling and risk analysis is key. AI roles in this sector often involve developing algorithms for trading, credit scoring, and fraud detection. In retail, experience with recommendation systems and customer analytics is highly beneficial. AI experts in this industry work to create personalized shopping experiences and optimize supply chain operations.

Interactive Element: AI Skills Self-Assessment

Take a moment to assess your current skills and identify areas for improvement. Answer the following questions to gauge where you stand and what you need to focus on:

1. Technical Skills:

- Are you proficient in machine learning frameworks like TensorFlow or PyTorch?
- How comfortable are you with data analysis and visualization tools such as Pandas and Tableau?
- Do you have a strong grasp of programming languages like Python or R?
- Can you explain neural network architectures and deep learning techniques?

2. Soft Skills:

- How would you rate your problem-solving and critical-thinking abilities?
- Are you comfortable working in a team and communicating complex ideas clearly?
- Do you embrace continuous learning and adapt to new technologies quickly?
- How do you approach ethical decision-making in your work?

3. Industry-Specific Skills:

- If you're interested in healthcare, do you have knowledge of medical imaging and health informatics?

- For finance, how well do you understand financial modeling and risk analysis?
- In retail, are you experienced with recommendation systems and customer analytics?

Reflect on your answers and make a plan to develop the skills you need to succeed in the AI job market. Whether enrolling in online courses, participating in workshops, or working on personal projects, taking proactive steps will help you build a strong foundation for a rewarding career in AI.

8.2 TRANSITIONING CAREERS: HOW TO PIVOT INTO AI ROLES

Imagine you're sitting at your desk, feeling unfulfilled in your current job, but you need help to make a change. Transitioning into an AI role might seem daunting, but it's more achievable than you think, especially if you can identify transferable skills from your current or previous roles. For example, your data analysis skills are highly relevant if you've worked in finance. You've likely spent time crunching numbers, identifying trends, and making data-driven decisions and skills that are invaluable in AI. Similarly, if you have programming experience from software development, you already possess a strong foundation in coding. This experience will help you quickly grasp machine learning frameworks and algorithms. Academic positions often require extensive research and problem-solving abilities, which are crucial in AI for developing new models and approaching complex challenges with innovative solutions.

Once you've identified your transferable skills, the next step is to reskill and upskill. There are numerous strategies to help you acquire the necessary skills and knowledge for AI roles. Enrolling in online AI courses and boot camps is a great place to start. Platforms like Coursera, Udacity, and edX offer courses ranging from introductory to advanced levels, often taught by industry experts. Participating in AI workshops and seminars can provide hands-on experience and networking opportunities with professionals. Engaging in self-study through books, tutorials, and online resources allows you to learn at your own pace. Additionally, taking on AI-related projects or internships gives you practical experience and a chance to apply what you've learned in real-world scenarios.

Building a transition plan is crucial for a smooth career shift into AI. Start by setting clear career goals and timelines. Define what you want to achieve and by when. For instance, aim to complete foundational courses within six months, followed by more specialized training. Identify your skill gaps and create a learning plan to address them. This might involve taking specific courses, working on targeted projects, or seeking mentorship. Networking with AI professionals and mentors can provide invaluable guidance and insights. Attend industry events, join online forums, and connect with experts on platforms like LinkedIn. Gaining practical experience through projects and collaborations is essential. Look for opportunities to work on AI initiatives within your current organization or volunteer for AI projects in the community.

To illustrate the possibilities, consider some success stories of individuals who transitioned into AI roles from different backgrounds. Take, for example, a marketing professional who pivoted to data science. Initially working with customer data for targeted marketing campaigns, they leveraged their analytical skills and enrolled in an online data science boot camp. Through dedicated learning and hands-on projects, they gained proficiency in machine learning and eventually secured a data scientist role. Another case is a mechanical engineer who transitioned to AI in robotics. With a background in designing mechanical systems, they pursued additional education in AI and robotics, applying their engineering skills to develop intelligent robotic solutions. Then there's the story of a teacher who moved into AI education and curriculum development. Passionate about teaching and technology, they combined their classroom experience with AI training to create educational programs that integrate AI concepts, empowering the next generation of learners.

These stories highlight that a career transition into AI is possible and rewarding. You can successfully pivot into an AI role by identifying your transferable skills, committing to reskilling and upskilling and building a structured transition plan. Whether you come from finance, engineering, marketing, or education, the AI field offers diverse opportunities for those willing to learn and adapt. The key is to take proactive steps, seek out learning resources, and connect with the AI community. With dedication and the right strategy, you can navigate this career shift and find fulfillment in the dynamic world of AI.

8.3 AI CERTIFICATIONS: BOOSTING YOUR RESUME

AI certifications can significantly enhance your career prospects and credibility in the competitive job market. Think of certifications as official stamps of your expertise, signaling to employers that you possess the necessary skills and knowledge. These certifications validate your proficiency in various AI domains, making you a more attractive candidate. For instance, having a certification in TensorFlow or PyTorch demonstrates your hands-on experience with these essential machine learning frameworks. Employers often seek certified professionals because it reduces the risk associated with hiring, assuring them that you have undergone rigorous training and assessment.

Several well-recognized AI certification programs can help boost your resume. Google's TensorFlow Developer Certificate is highly regarded for validating your ability to build and deploy machine learning models using TensorFlow. This certification is particularly beneficial if you aim to work in tech companies or startups focused on AI-driven products. IBM offers the AI Engineering Professional Certificate, which covers a broad spectrum of AI topics, from machine learning to deep learning and NLP. This certification is ideal for those looking to enter diverse industries, including healthcare and finance. Microsoft's Azure AI Engineer Associate Certification focuses on designing and implementing AI solutions on the Azure platform, making it perfect for roles in companies using cloud-based AI services. Coursera's Machine Learning Specialization by Andrew Ng is another excellent option, offering a deep dive into machine learning fundamentals and applications. This specialization enhances your theoretical knowledge and provides practical skills, making you job-ready.

Preparing for AI certification exams requires a strategic approach and dedication. Start by studying the exam syllabus and objectives to understand the topics covered and the skills assessed. Official study materials and courses are invaluable resources, providing structured content and practice exercises. Practicing with sample questions and mock exams helps you familiarize yourself with the exam format and identify areas for improvement. Joining study groups and online forums can also be beneficial. These communities offer support, share resources, and provide insights from individuals who have already taken the exams. Engaging with peers can motivate you and help clarify complex topics. Utilizing official study guides, video tutorials, and hands-on projects ensures you comprehensively understand the material.

Once you've obtained your certifications, effectively showcasing them on your resume and during job interviews is crucial.

Highlight your certifications prominently in the skills and education sections of your resume. Include details about the certification, such as the issuing organization and the completion date. During interviews, discuss the projects and practical experiences you gained while preparing for the certifications. For example, if you built a predictive model using TensorFlow, explain the project's objectives, your approach, and the outcome. Demonstrating the practical applications of your certified skills can set you apart from other candidates. Employers appreciate candidates who can translate theoretical knowledge into real-world solutions. Additionally, certifications can be conversation starters, allowing you to delve deeper into your expertise and enthusiasm for AI during interviews.

As you navigate your AI career, remember that certifications are not just about adding credentials to your resume. They represent your commitment to learning and staying updated in a rapidly evolving field. Being certified shows that you're proactive and dedicated to your professional growth. It's an investment in your future, opening doors to new opportunities and career advancement. Whether you're just starting or looking to advance in your AI career, certifications can be a powerful tool to validate your skills and enhance your marketability.

8.4 NETWORKING IN THE AI COMMUNITY: BUILDING CONNECTIONS

Picture yourself at a bustling tech event, mingling with professionals who share your passion for AI. The conversations are rich with insights, and each interaction presents a new opportunity. Networking within the AI community is more than just exchanging business cards; it's about building relationships that can propel your career forward. By connecting with others, you gain insights into the latest industry trends, discover job openings, and even find project collaborators. Networking opens doors to opportunities that you might not find through traditional job-searching methods. It's a way to stay updated with the rapid advancements in AI and to keep your skills relevant.

There are numerous avenues for networking, both online and offline. LinkedIn is a powerful tool for connecting with AI professionals. By joining AI-focused groups, you can engage in discussions, share articles, and learn from others' experiences. AI conferences and meetups are invaluable for face-to-face interactions. Events like NeurIPS or local AI meetups provide a platform to meet industry leaders and peers. Online forums such as Reddit's r/MachineLearning and Stack Overflow are great for asking questions, sharing knowledge, and solving problems collaboratively. Professional organizations like the Association for the Advancement of Artificial Intelligence (AAAI) offer memberships that include access to exclusive events, publications, and networking opportunities.

Building a personal brand in the AI community can set you apart and make you more recognizable. Start by creating and sharing AI-related content on social media. Whether it's a blog post about a recent AI breakthrough or a tutorial on a machine learning technique, sharing your knowledge demonstrates your expertise. Contributing to open-source AI projects on platforms like GitHub enhances your skills and showcases your work to potential employers. Writing articles and blogs on AI topics can establish you as a thought leader. You can even consider speaking at conferences and webinars. Public speaking boosts your visibility and builds your confidence and communication skills.

Finding mentors and collaborators is crucial for your growth in the AI field. A mentor can provide guidance, share valuable insights, and help you navigate your career path. Joining mentorship programs offered by professional organizations or tech companies can connect you with experienced AI professionals. Don't hesitate to reach out to AI experts for advice and guidance. Most professionals are willing to share their knowledge and experiences. Collaborating on AI research and projects can also be beneficial. Working with others allows you to learn new techniques, gain different perspectives, and produce more robust solutions. Participating in AI hackathons and competitions is another excellent way to meet like-minded individuals and potential collaborators. These events encourage teamwork and innovation, providing a platform to showcase your skills and creativity.

Imagine you've just completed a machine learning course and are eager to apply your knowledge. You join a local AI meetup and meet someone working on a similar project. This connection leads to a collaboration, where you both learn from each other and create something impressive. Such opportunities arise from being active in the AI community. Networking is not just about what others can offer you; it's also about what you can contribute. Sharing your experiences, offering help, and being genuinely interested in others' work creates a positive impression. Over time, these interactions build a network of supportive and resourceful contacts that can significantly impact your career.

Networking in the AI community is a continuous process that requires effort and genuine interest. By actively participating in discussions, attending events, building your brand, and seeking mentors and collaborators, you create a solid foundation for your career. The AI field is evolving rapidly, and staying connected with the community ensures you are always at the forefront of the latest developments.

8.5 CRAFTING A CAREER PLAN: STEPS TO ACHIEVE YOUR AI GOALS

Setting clear career goals is the first step in crafting a successful career plan in AI. You must set specific, measurable, achievable, relevant, and time-bound (SMART) goals to provide direction and motivation. Start by identifying the job roles and industries that excite you. Are you drawn to healthcare and fascinated by the potential of AI to revolutionize diagnostics? Or perhaps the financial sector intrigues you, with its cutting-edge fraud detection systems. Once you have a clear vision of your desired role, set short-term and long-term milestones. Short-term goals could include completing an introductory AI course or building a simple machine learning model. Long-term goals might involve securing a position as a data scientist or developing an AI-driven project. Align these goals with your personal interests and strengths to ensure they remain motivating and achievable.

Creating a skills development plan is crucial once you have set your career goals. Start by listing the technical and soft skills required for your target roles. For instance, proficiency in machine learning frameworks like TensorFlow and PyTorch, programming languages like Python, and data analysis tools like Pandas are essential technical skills. Critical thinking, problem-solving, and effective communication are invaluable on the soft skills side. Identify relevant courses, certifications, and resources to help you acquire these skills. Enroll in online courses, participate in workshops, and read authoritative books on AI. Allocate dedicated time for learning and practice, ensuring you balance skill acquisition with your current responsibilities. Track your progress regularly, adjusting your plan as needed to address any skill gaps or new opportunities that arise.

Gaining practical experience is a cornerstone of any successful AI career plan. More than theory alone will be required; you need hands-on experience to solidify your knowledge and demonstrate your capabilities. Start by working on personal AI projects that align with your interests. Whether it's developing a chatbot or creating a predictive model, these projects provide valuable learning experiences and portfolio material. Internships and co-op programs offer structured, real-world experience and mentorship from industry professionals. Collaborate with peers on AI research or community projects, leveraging collective knowledge to tackle complex problems. Contributing to open-source AI projects is another excellent way to gain practical experience while making meaningful contributions to the AI community.

Continuously evaluating and adapting your career plan is essential to stay on track and capitalize on new opportunities. Conduct periodic self-assessments to gauge your progress toward your goals. Are you meeting your milestones? Are there areas where you need to improve or focus more? Seek feedback from mentors, peers, and industry professionals to gain different perspectives on your development. Stay updated with industry trends and advancements by reading research papers, attending conferences, and participating in online forums. The AI field evolves rapidly, and being aware of the latest developments ensures your skills and knowledge remain relevant. Adjust your goals and strategies as needed, staying flexible and open to new opportunities that align with your career aspirations.

By setting clear career goals, creating a comprehensive skills development plan, gaining practical experience, and continuously evaluating and adapting your approach, you lay a solid foundation for a successful career in AI. The journey may be challenging, but with dedication and a well-structured plan, you can navigate the dynamic landscape of AI and achieve your professional goals. As you move forward, remember that the AI field is constantly evolving, offering endless opportunities for those who are willing to learn and adapt. Stay curious, stay motivated, and continue to build on your knowledge and experience.

In the next chapter, we will explore the resources available for continuous learning in AI, ensuring you have access to the tools and knowledge needed to stay ahead in this rapidly evolving field.

Interactive Quiz: Career Prospects in AI

1. AI in the Job Market: Skills in Demand

Question: Which of the following is one of the most in-demand technical skills for AI professionals?

- a) Event planning
- b) Python programming
- c) Public speaking

Question: What is an example of a soft skill that employers value in AI roles?

- a) Experience with neural networks
- b) Strong communication skills
- c) Knowledge of TensorFlow

2. Transitioning Careers: How to Pivot into AI Roles

Question: Which transferable skill can help someone pivot into an AI role from a non-technical background?

- a) Public speaking
- b) Data analysis

c) Event coordination

Question: What is one of the most effective ways to gain practical experience when transitioning into an AI career?

a) Reading AI blogs
b) Contributing to open-source AI projects
c) Following AI influencers on social media

3. AI Certifications: Boosting Your Resume

Question: Which of the following certifications is offered by Google?

a) IBM AI Engineering Professional Certificate
b) TensorFlow Developer Certificate
c) Microsoft Azure AI Engineer Associate Certification

Question: Why are AI certifications valuable for your career?

a) They prove you have extensive work experience.
b) They validate your skills and knowledge in specific AI domains.
c) They are required by all employers.

4. Networking in the AI Community: Building Connections

Question: What is one benefit of attending AI conferences or meetups?

a) Learning about unrelated industries
b) Building connections and discovering job opportunities
c) Avoiding professional networking

Question: Which platform is mentioned as effective for connecting with AI professionals online?

a) Instagram
b) LinkedIn
c) Pinterest

5. Crafting a Career Plan: Steps to Achieve Your AI Goals

Question: What is the first step in crafting a successful AI career plan?

a) Setting clear career goals
b) Buying AI books
c) Avoiding new technologies

Question: How can you continuously evaluate and adapt your career plan?

a) Ignoring industry trends
b) Conducting periodic self-assessments and seeking feedback
c) Sticking to one strategy permanently

9

RESOURCES FOR CONTINUOUS LEARNING

I magine sitting at your favorite café, sipping a hot cup of coffee while you scroll through your smartphone, pondering how to dive into the world of AI. You feel a mix of excitement and apprehension, knowing that AI is rapidly changing the world but unsure how to start learning it. Fortunately, the internet offers many resources tailored to different learning styles and paces. One of the most accessible and versatile ways to learn AI is through online courses and MOOCs (Massive Open Online Courses). These platforms allow you to learn at your own pace, fitting education into your busy life without the constraints of traditional classrooms.

Online learning platforms like Coursera, edX, Udacity, and Khan Academy have revolutionized education by providing high-quality courses from top universities and industry experts. Coursera, for instance, partners with leading institutions like Stanford and Google to offer courses that range from introductory to advanced levels. edX, founded by Harvard and MIT, provides similar courses, including verified certificates that can bolster your resume. Udacity focuses on industry-relevant skills, often collaborating with tech giants to create "Nanodegree" programs that prepare you for specific job roles. Though less specialized in AI, Khan Academy offers foundational computer science and mathematics courses, which are crucial for understanding AI concepts.

If you're beginning your AI journey, several highly-rated introductory courses can help you get started. Andrew Ng's "Machine Learning" course on Coursera is a popular choice that has introduced thousands of learners to the fundamentals of machine learning. Another excellent option is "AI For Everyone," also by Andrew Ng on Coursera, which demystifies AI and explains its applications in a non-technical manner. For a broader overview, the "Introduction to Artificial Intelligence" course by IBM on edX provides a comprehensive introduction to AI principles, ethics, and applications. These courses are designed to be accessible, breaking down complex topics into digestible lessons and offering practical exercises to reinforce learning.

As you gain confidence and knowledge, you might want to delve deeper into specialized AI topics. Coursera's "Deep Learning Specialization," which Andrew Ng created, covers neural networks, convolutional networks, sequence models, and more. This series of courses is ideal for those looking to understand the intricacies of deep learning. "AI for Medicine Specialization" on Coursera is another advanced course that applies AI techniques to medical data, focusing on diagnostics, treatment planning, and medical imaging. For those interested in autonomous vehicles, the "Self-Driving Car Engineer Nanodegree" on Udacity offers a detailed curriculum covering everything from computer vision to sensor fusion, preparing you for a career in the burgeoning field of autonomous driving.

Learning at your own pace requires discipline and effective strategies to stay on track. One crucial tip is setting a consistent study schedule that fits your daily routine. Whether it's an hour every morning or a few evenings a week, consistency helps reinforce learning and makes it a habit. Breaking down courses into manageable sections prevents overwhelm and allows you to focus on one topic at a time. Joining study groups or forums can provide peer support and motivation. Platforms like Coursera and edX often have discussion boards where you can interact with fellow learners, ask questions, and share insights.

Self-Paced Learning Checklist

1. Set a Consistent Study Schedule: Allocate specific times each week dedicated to your AI courses.
2. Break Down Courses: Divide the course into smaller sections or modules. Focus on completing one section at a time.

3. Join Study Groups: Participate in online forums or study groups related to your course.

4. Set Goals: Define clear, achievable goals for each study session. For example, aim to complete a particular module or understand a specific concept.

5. Celebrate Milestones: Reward yourself for reaching milestones, such as completing a course or passing an assessment.

6. Stay Active: Engage with the course material by taking notes, completing exercises, and applying what you learn to real-world problems.

By leveraging these online resources and strategies, you can effectively navigate the expansive world of AI, learning at a pace that suits you best.

9.1 AI BOOKS AND PUBLICATIONS: MUST-READS FOR ENTHUSIASTS

Picture yourself in a cozy reading nook with a stack of books that promise to unravel the mysteries of AI. For beginners, diving into the right books can make all the difference. "Artificial Intelligence: A Guide for Thinking Humans" by Melanie Mitchell is a fantastic starting point. Mitchell uses engaging narratives and real-world examples to explain complex AI concepts in a way that's easy to understand. Another gem is "Life 3.0: Being Human in the Age of Artificial Intelligence" by Max Tegmark. This book explores the future impact of AI on society, providing a thought-provoking look at how AI could reshape our world. If you're curious about the global AI race, "AI Superpowers: China, Silicon Valley, and the New World Order" by Kai-Fu Lee offers an insightful analysis of how China and the U.S. are leading the charge in AI development and what this means for the future.

You can tackle more advanced topics as you become more comfortable with the basics. "Deep Learning" by Ian Goodfellow, Yoshua Bengio, and Aaron Courville is often considered the bible of deep learning. This comprehensive guide delves into the theory and practice of neural networks and is essential for anyone serious about mastering deep learning. For a broader look at machine learning techniques, "Pattern Recognition and Machine Learning" by Christopher Bishop thoroughly introduces the field, covering everything from basic algorithms to advanced topics like Bayesian networks. If you prefer a more hands-on approach, "Hands-On Machine Learning with Scikit-Learn, Keras, and TensorFlow" by Aurélien Géron is an excellent choice. This book walks you through the practical aspects of implementing machine learning models using popular libraries, complete with code examples and exercises.

Staying updated with the latest research is crucial in a field as dynamic as AI. Reputable journals and publications offer a wealth of knowledge and are invaluable resources for anyone keen on keeping up with advancements. The "Journal of Artificial Intelligence Research (JAIR)" publishes cutting-edge research across all areas of AI, from machine learning to natural language processing. "IEEE Transactions on Neural Networks and Learning Systems" focuses on neural networks, providing insights into their theoretical and practical aspects. For a broader scope, the "Machine Learning Journal" covers a wide range of topics, from foundational research to applications in various industries. Subscribing to these journals can keep you informed about the latest breakthroughs and trends, helping you stay ahead of the curve.

To get the most out of your reading, consider adopting some effective strategies for comprehension and retention. Active reading techniques, such as summarizing key points and asking questions, can help you engage more deeply with the material. Taking notes and creating mind maps are excellent ways to visualize and organize complex information, making it easier to recall later. Discussing key concepts with peers or mentors can also enhance your understanding, as teaching others is one of the best ways to solidify your knowledge. These practices can turn reading from a passive activity into an interactive learning experience, ensuring you grasp and retain the valuable insights these books and journals offer.

Interactive Element: Recommended Reading List

1. Beginners:

- "Artificial Intelligence: A Guide for Thinking Humans" by Melanie Mitchell
- "Life 3.0: Being Human in the Age of Artificial Intelligence" by Max Tegmark
- "AI Superpowers: China, Silicon Valley, and the New World Order" by Kai-Fu Lee

2. Advanced Learners:

- "Deep Learning" by Ian Goodfellow, Yoshua Bengio, and Aaron Courville
- "Pattern Recognition and Machine Learning" by Christopher Bishop
- "Hands-On Machine Learning with Scikit-Learn, Keras, and TensorFlow" by Aurélien Géron

3. Research Journals:

- "Journal of Artificial Intelligence Research (JAIR)"
- "IEEE Transactions on Neural Networks and Learning Systems"
- "Machine Learning Journal"

By diving into these books and publications, you'll find yourself well-equipped to navigate the fascinating world of AI.

9.2 AI CONFERENCES AND WORKSHOPS: ENGAGING WITH THE COMMUNITY

Imagine walking into a bustling conference hall filled with people who share your passion for AI. The energy is infectious, and you can feel the excitement in the air. Attending AI conferences and workshops offers a unique opportunity to immerse yourself in the latest advancements, network with professionals, and learn directly from experts. These events provide a platform to discover cutting-edge research, gain insights into industry trends, and even find potential collaborators for your projects. The knowledge and connections you gain can be invaluable, helping you stay ahead in this rapidly evolving field.

NeurIPS (Conference on Neural Information Processing Systems) is one of the most influential AI conferences. It's renowned for presenting groundbreaking research in machine learning and computational neuroscience. ICML (International Conference on Machine Learning) is another major event that attracts top researchers and practitioners from around the world. CVPR (Conference on Computer Vision and Pattern Recognition) focuses on the latest developments in computer vision, making it a must-attend for anyone interested in image recognition and related technologies. The AAAI Conference on Artificial Intelligence covers a broad spectrum of AI topics, offering diverse sessions that cater to various interests and expertise levels. Attending these conferences can provide a comprehensive view of the state of AI, from theoretical advancements to practical applications.

If attending major conferences isn't feasible, virtual and regional AI events offer accessible alternatives. AI webinars and online workshops bring expert knowledge directly to your screen, allowing you to learn from the comfort of your home. Local AI meetups and hackathons provide opportunities to connect with nearby enthusiasts and work on collaborative projects. Virtual summits and conferences have also become more prevalent, offering interactive sessions, live Q&A, and networking opportunities without the need for travel. These events ensure you stay connected and informed, regardless of location or schedule.

Preparation is key to making the most out of attending AI conferences and workshops. Start by reviewing the agenda and selecting sessions that align with your interests. Planning ahead helps you focus on the most relevant talks and workshops, maximizing your learning experience. Networking with speakers and other attendees can open doors to new opportunities and collaborations. Don't hesitate to introduce yourself and share your interests; these interactions can lead to valuable connections and insights. Participating in Q&A sessions and panel discussions allows you to engage with the content actively and gain a deeper understanding. Following up with contacts after the event is essential for building lasting relationships. Send a quick message or email to express your appreciation and keep the conversation going.

Interactive Element: Maximizing Your Conference Experience

1. Plan Ahead: Review the conference agenda and select sessions that align with your interests.
2. Network Actively: Introduce yourself to speakers and attendees, sharing your interests and goals.
3. Engage in Q&A: Participate in Q&A sessions and panel discussions to deepen your understanding.
4. Follow Up: Send follow-up messages or emails to contacts you met, expressing your appreciation and interest in staying connected.

Attending AI conferences and workshops can be transformative, providing you with the knowledge, inspiration, and connections needed to thrive in AI. Whether attending a major event like NeurIPS or joining a local meetup, these experiences enrich your learning and open doors to new possibilities.

9.3 PODCASTS AND WEBINARS: LISTENING TO AI EXPERTS

Imagine you're walking your dog or cooking dinner, and you want to stay updated on the latest AI trends but need more time to sit down with a book or attend a conference. This is where AI podcasts come in handy. They offer a convenient way to absorb new information and insights while you go about your daily routine. AI podcasts feature interviews with experts, discussions on recent advancements, and insights into the future of AI. They are perfect for making the most of your time, whether commuting, exercising, or just relaxing at home. Listening to these podcasts can help you stay informed about the latest trends, breakthroughs, and debates in the AI community without requiring a dedicated time slot in your busy schedule.

Several AI podcasts have gained popularity for their valuable content and engaging format. "The TWIML AI Podcast (This Week in Machine Learning & AI)" is a fantastic resource that covers a wide range of topics, from deep learning and natural language processing to AI ethics and policy. Hosted by Sam Charrington, it features interviews with leading experts, providing a deep dive into their work and perspectives. Another excellent podcast is the "AI Alignment Podcast" by the Future of Life Institute, which discusses AI's ethical and existential risks. Rob Miles also hosts an insightful "AI Alignment Podcast" that delves into how we can align AI systems with human values. For those interested in data science and its applications, "Data Skeptic" offers a mix of interviews and solo episodes that explore the intersection of AI, data science, and skepticism.

Webinars and online talks are another excellent way to stay current with AI developments. The "AI for Good Global Summit webinars" bring together experts from various fields to discuss how AI can be leveraged for social good. These webinars cover topics like AI in healthcare, climate change, and humanitarian efforts. The "Stanford AI Lab talks" are also highly regarded, offering insights from one of the leading AI research institutions. Webinars hosted by AI research institutions and companies provide a wealth of knowledge and often feature the latest research findings and technological advancements. TED Talks on AI is another valuable resource, offering concise and impactful presentations on various aspects of artificial intelligence by prominent thinkers and innovators.

It's helpful to adopt some effective listening and engagement strategies to get the most out of AI podcasts and webinars. Taking notes during episodes or talks can help you retain key points and revisit them later. It's also beneficial to join live webinars whenever possible, allowing you to participate in Q&A sessions and engage directly with the speakers. Discussing key takeaways with peers or in online forums can deepen your understanding and provide different perspectives on the topics covered. Applying insights gained to your personal projects or studies can make the content more relevant and practical, reinforcing your learning through real-world application.

Tips for Effective Listening and Engagement

1. Take Notes: Jot down key points, interesting ideas, and questions that arise during the podcast or webinar.
2. Join Live Webinars: Participate in Q&A sessions to clarify doubts and engage with the speaker.
3. Discuss Key Takeaways: Share and discuss what you've learned with peers or in online forums to gain different perspectives.
4. Apply Insights: Use the knowledge gained in your personal projects or studies to reinforce learning through practical application.

By incorporating these strategies, you can transform passive listening into an active learning experience, making the most of the valuable content offered by AI podcasts and webinars.

9.4 CURATED RESOURCE LISTS: TOOLS AND WEBSITES FOR DEEP DIVES

Imagine you're sitting at your desk, eager to expand your knowledge of AI beyond just courses and books. The internet is a treasure trove of resources that can take your understanding to the next level. Comprehensive AI resource lists are a great way to access various information, tools, and tutorials. Websites like Towards Data Science and KDnuggets offer extensive articles, tutorials, and resource lists covering foundational concepts and cutting-edge research. These platforms curate content from experts, providing insights that range from beginner-friendly explanations to advanced techniques. Educational resources on platforms like DeepAI and Fast.ai also offer specialized courses and tutorials, diving deep into various AI topics. These sites are invaluable for continuous learning and staying updated with the latest trends and technologies in AI.

Interactive learning platforms offer a hands-on approach to mastering AI. Kaggle, for instance, is a favorite among data scientists for its practical challenges and competition. Participating in Kaggle challenges allows you to apply your skills to real-world problems, collaborate with other enthusiasts, and learn from detailed solutions the community shares. Google Colab is another fantastic tool that allows you to write and execute Python code in your browser, making it easy to experiment with AI models and algorithms. Colab supports various AI libraries and offers free access to powerful GPUs, enabling you to train complex models without needing a high-end computer. AI Playground is a fun and interactive platform where you can experiment with different AI models and see their outputs in real time. These platforms make learning AI engaging and practical, helping you bridge the gap between theory and application.

When it comes to specialized AI tools and libraries, having the right resources at your fingertips can significantly enhance your learning and projects. TensorFlow and PyTorch are two of the most popular deep learning frameworks widely used by researchers and practitioners alike. TensorFlow, developed by Google, offers a robust ecosystem for building and deploying machine learning models, while PyTorch, developed by Facebook, is known for its flexibility and ease of use. Scikit-learn is a go-to library for machine learning in Python, providing simple and efficient data mining and analysis tools. NLTK (Natural Language Toolkit) and SpaCy are indispensable for natural language processing. NLTK is great for educational purposes and offers a wide range of text-processing libraries, while SpaCy is designed for production use and excels in performance. These tools and libraries are essential for anyone serious about diving deep into AI, offering the building blocks for creating sophisticated models and applications.

Community and support forums are invaluable for troubleshooting, learning, and connecting with like-minded individuals. Stack Overflow is a well-known platform where you can ask coding and technical questions and receive answers from a vast community of developers and experts. It's a great place to get quick help and learn from others' experiences. Reddit's r/MachineLearning and r/artificial are active communities where enthusiasts and professionals discuss AI topics, share resources, and provide support. These subreddits are excellent for staying updated on the latest developments, asking questions, and engaging in meaningful discussions. AI-specific Discord servers and Slack channels offer real-time communication and are often organized around specific topics or projects. These platforms provide collaboration, mentorship, and networking opportunities, making them essential for anyone looking to immerse themselves in the AI community.

Engaging with these curated resources, interactive platforms, specialized tools, and supportive communities will deepen your understanding of AI and keep you motivated and inspired. The wealth of knowledge available at your fingertips makes it easier than ever to explore the fascinating world of AI and apply what you learn to real-world problems.

By leveraging these diverse resources, you'll find yourself well-equipped to navigate the complexities of AI, gaining the skills and insights needed to thrive.

Interactive Quiz: Resources for Continuous Learning

1. Online Courses and MOOCs

Question: Which of the following platforms offers industry-focused "Nanodegree" programs specifically tailored for AI job roles?

  a) Coursera
  b) Khan Academy
  c) Udacity

Question: What is a key strategy for successful self-paced learning in AI?

  a) Skipping challenging sections
  b) Setting a consistent study schedule
  c) Watching videos without taking notes

2. AI Books and Publications

Question: Which book is recommended for beginners interested in understanding AI concepts in a relatable way?

  a) "Deep Learning" by Ian Goodfellow
  b) "Artificial Intelligence: A Guide for Thinking Humans" by Melanie Mitchell
  c) "Pattern Recognition and Machine Learning" by Christopher Bishop

Question: What is the focus of the "Journal of Artificial Intelligence Research (JAIR)"?

a) Exploring AI applications in entertainment
b) Publishing cutting-edge AI research across various domains
c) Analyzing the impact of AI on economic policies

3. AI Conferences and Workshops

Question: Which major AI conference is known for its focus on machine learning and computational neuroscience?

a) NeurIPS
b) CES
c) TEDx

Question: What is an effective way to maximize your experience at an AI conference?

a) Skipping Q&A sessions
b) Networking actively with attendees and speakers
c) Attending only one session per day

4. Podcasts and Webinars

Question: Which podcast is known for covering a wide range of AI topics, from deep learning to AI ethics?

a) "Data Skeptic"
b) "The TWIML AI Podcast"
c) "Stuff You Should Know"

Question: How can you enhance your engagement while listening to AI podcasts?

a) Listen passively without taking notes
b) Discuss key takeaways with peers or in forums
c) Skip episodes that cover unfamiliar topics

5. Curated Resource Lists and Tools

Question: Which platform allows you to participate in AI challenges and collaborate with other data scientists?

a) Stack Overflow
b) Kaggle
c) Google Scholar

Question: What is the primary advantage of using interactive platforms like Google Colab for AI learning?

a) Limited access to AI libraries
b) Free access to powerful computing resources
c) Lack of support for code execution

10

SPECIAL TOPICS IN AI

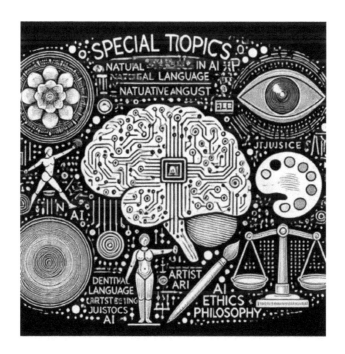

Imagine you're at a bustling airport, surrounded by travelers from all over the world. You see signs in multiple languages, hear announcements in different dialects, and watch as people communicate in various tongues. In all this chaos, your smartphone seamlessly translates a sign for you and helps you navigate a foreign land. This incredible feat is made possible by Natural Language Processing (NLP), a field of AI that allows computers to understand, interpret, and generate human language.

10.1 NATURAL LANGUAGE PROCESSING (NLP): AI'S UNDERSTANDING OF HUMAN LANGUAGE

Natural Language Processing, or NLP, is a branch of AI that focuses on interactions between computers and human languages. At its core, NLP enables machines to process and analyze large amounts of natural language data, which can include anything from text to spoken words. NLP's significance lies in its ability to bridge the gap between human communication and computer understanding. By doing so, it allows AI systems to perform tasks that involve language, such as translation, sentiment analysis, and even generating coherent text.

One of the fundamental techniques in NLP is tokenization. Tokenization involves breaking down text into smaller units, such as individual words or phrases. This is like dissecting a sentence into its building blocks, making it easier for a computer to analyze and understand. For example, the sentence "The quick brown fox jumps over the lazy dog" would be tokenized into ["The," "quick," "brown," "fox," "jumps," "over," "the," "lazy," "dog"]. Each token represents a piece of the puzzle that the AI needs to solve.

Another essential technique is Part-of-Speech (POS) tagging, which identifies the grammatical categories of words within a text. This allows the AI to understand the function of each word in a sentence. For instance, in the sentence "She sells seashells by the seashore," POS tagging would identify "She" as a pronoun, "sells" as a verb, and "seashells" as a noun. By understanding the roles of these words, the AI can grasp the sentence's structure and meaning.

Named Entity Recognition (NER) is another crucial technique in NLP. NER involves detecting and classifying entities within a text, such as names of people, organizations, locations, and dates. For example, in the sentence "Barack Obama was born in Hawaii," NER would identify "Barack Obama" as a person and "Hawaii" as a location. This allows the AI to recognize and differentiate between various entities, enhancing its understanding of the text.

Sentiment analysis is a widely used NLP technique that determines the emotional tone of a piece of text. It can identify whether the sentiment is positive, negative, or neutral. For instance, a product review stating, "I love this phone! It has fantastic battery life and a sleek design," would be classified as a positive sentiment. Businesses often use sentiment analysis to gauge customer opinions and feedback, allowing them to make informed decisions.

NLP has numerous real-world applications that have transformed various industries. Chatbots and virtual assistants like Siri and Alexa rely on NLP to understand and respond to user queries. These AI-powered assistants can answer questions, set reminders, and even control smart home devices, making daily tasks more manageable. Language translation services like Google Translate use NLP to break down language barriers by translating text and speech between different languages. This has made communication across cultures more accessible and efficient.

Text summarization tools are another application of NLP. They help users quickly grasp the main points of lengthy documents by providing concise summaries. For instance, summarization tools can condense a lengthy news article into a few key sentences, making it easier for readers to stay informed without spending too much time. Speech recognition and transcription services also rely on NLP to convert spoken language into written text. This technology is widely used in applications like voice-to-text features on smartphones and automated transcription services for meetings and interviews.

Recent advancements in NLP have led to significant breakthroughs and trends in the field. One such breakthrough is the development of transformers and attention mechanisms. Transformers are a type of neural network architecture that has revolutionized NLP by allowing models to process entire text sequences simultaneously rather than word by word. This enables the AI to understand the context and relationships between words more effectively. Attention mechanisms, on the other hand, help the model focus on specific parts of the input text, improving its ability to capture relevant information.

BERT (Bidirectional Encoder Representations from Transformers) is a state-of-the-art NLP model that has set new benchmarks in various NLP tasks. BERT's bidirectional approach allows it to consider the context from both the left and right sides of a word, making it highly effective in understanding the nuances of language. This has significantly improved tasks such as question-answering, text classification, and language inference.

Another groundbreaking model is GPT-4 (Generative Pre-trained Transformer 4), developed by OpenAI. With 175 billion parameters, GPT-4 is one of the largest and most powerful language models ever created. It can generate coherent and contextually relevant text based on a given prompt, making it capable of tasks like writing essays, composing poetry, and even generating code. GPT-4's ability to generate human-like text has opened up new possibilities for creative applications and automated content creation.

Multilingual NLP models have also seen significant advancements, allowing AI systems to understand and generate text in multiple languages. These models can perform cross-lingual tasks, such as translating text from one language to another, while maintaining the context and meaning. This has further enhanced the accessibility and usability of NLP technologies globally, breaking down language barriers and facilitating communication across cultures.

NLP's potential is vast, and its applications continue to expand as technology advances. From understanding human language to generating coherent text, NLP transforms how we interact with machines and makes AI more accessible and intuitive. The developments in NLP are technical achievements and pave the way for more inclusive and connected experiences in our increasingly digital world.

10.2 GENERATIVE AI: CREATING NEW CONTENT WITH AI

Imagine scrolling through social media and coming across a stunning piece of digital art. The colors are vibrant, the details meticulous, and the style reminiscent of a famous artist. You're captivated, but what surprises you more is that this artwork was created by an AI, not by a human. This is the realm of generative AI, a fascinating field of artificial intelligence that focuses on creating new content by learning patterns from existing data. Generative AI systems can produce text, images, music, and even videos, pushing the boundaries of creativity and innovation.

Generative AI is significant because it enables machines to generate content that is not only coherent but also creative. By learning from vast datasets, these AI systems can mimic styles, predict patterns, and create original pieces that can be indistinguishable from human-made content. This ability to generate new content has profound implications across various fields, from entertainment to education and beyond.

One of the core techniques in generative AI is the use of Generative Adversarial Networks (GANs). GANs consist of two neural networks, the generator, and the discriminator, that work in tandem. The generator creates new data points while the discriminator evaluates them for authenticity. This adversarial process continues until the generator produces highly realistic data that the discriminator can no longer distinguish from the real data. GANs have been instrumental in generating realistic images and videos, making them a powerful digital art and entertainment tool.

Another key technique is Variational Autoencoders (VAEs). VAEs are designed to generate new data points by learning the underlying distribution of the input data. They consist of an encoder that compresses the input data into a latent space and a decoder that reconstructs the data from this latent space. VAEs can generate new, similar data points by sampling from this latent space. This technique is particularly useful in creating variations of existing images or generating entirely new images based on learned patterns.

Recurrent Neural Networks (RNNs) are also essential in generative AI, especially for tasks involving sequences, such as text and music generation. RNNs are designed to handle sequential data by maintaining a memory of previous inputs, allowing them to generate coherent sequences. For example, an RNN can be trained on a dataset of musical compositions and then generate new pieces of music that follow the learned musical patterns. Similarly, RNNs can produce text that flows naturally, making them valuable for writing assistance and content creation.

Transformers significantly advance generative AI, particularly in natural language processing. Transformers leverage attention mechanisms to process entire text sequences simultaneously, capturing context and relationships between words more effectively. This has led to the development of state-of-the-art language models like GPT-4 (Generative Pre-trained Transformer 4). GPT-4 can generate human-like text based on a given prompt, making it capable of tasks like writing essays, composing poetry, and generating code. Its ability to produce coherent and contextually relevant text has opened up new possibilities for creative applications and automated content creation.

Generative AI has numerous real-world applications that are transforming various industries. For instance, AI-generated art and digital paintings are gaining popularity in the art world. Artists collaborate with AI systems to create unique pieces that blend human creativity with machine precision. These AI-generated artworks are showcased in galleries and sold at auctions, challenging traditional notions of creativity and authorship.

In music composition, AI tools like OpenAI's MuseNet can generate original music pieces by analyzing vast collections of musical data. These AI systems can compose melodies, harmonies, and full arrangements in different styles and genres, providing musicians with new ideas and inspiration. This has led to collaborations between AI and human musicians, resulting in innovative and experimental compositions.

Text generation is another significant application of generative AI. AI-powered writing assistants can help authors, journalists, and content creators by generating text based on given prompts. These tools can draft articles, create marketing copy, and even assist in writing novels. For example, an AI writing assistant can generate a first draft of an article, which the human writer can then edit and refine. This speeds up the writing process and allows for more efficient content creation.

Deepfake technology, which uses generative AI to create realistic videos and images, is also gaining attention. Deepfakes can superimpose one person's face onto another's body or create entirely synthetic videos that appear authentic. While this technology has potential applications in entertainment, such as creating realistic visual effects in movies, it raises ethical concerns. The ability to create convincing fake videos can lead to misuse, such as spreading misinformation or creating non-consensual explicit content.

The rise of generative AI brings with it several ethical considerations and challenges. One of the primary issues is the question of originality and authorship. When AI generates content, who owns the rights to it? Is it the developer of the AI system, the person who provided the data, or the AI itself? These questions complicate the legal landscape and require new frameworks to address intellectual property rights in the age of AI-generated content.

Another significant challenge is the potential misuse of deepfake technology. The ability to create realistic but fake videos can be exploited for malicious purposes, such as spreading false information or damaging reputations. Ensuring the ethical use of generative AI involves implementing safeguards and regulations to prevent misuse and protect individuals' rights.

Ensuring fairness and avoiding bias in generated content is also a critical concern. AI systems learn from existing data, and if this data contains biases, the generated content may perpetuate these biases. For example, an AI-generated text might exhibit gender or racial biases present in the training data. Developers must take steps to mitigate biases by using diverse and representative datasets and implementing fairness algorithms.

Balancing creativity and ethical responsibility is essential as generative AI continues to evolve. While the technology offers exciting possibilities for innovation and artistic expression, it also requires thoughtful consideration of its ethical implications. Establishing guidelines for the responsible use of generative AI, promoting transparency in AI-generated content, and fostering collaboration between AI developers, artists, and ethicists are crucial steps in navigating this complex landscape.

10.3 AI IN ETHICS AND PHILOSOPHY: DEBATING AI'S ROLE IN SOCIETY

Imagine browsing your favorite news app and coming across an article discussing the latest AI technology that predicts criminal behavior. You feel a mixture of awe and unease. This duality captures the essence of AI ethics and philosophy. These fields explore AI technologies' moral, societal, and existential implications, addressing their impact on humanity. As AI becomes more integrated into our lives, it's crucial to consider what these systems can do and what they should do.

Privacy and data protection are among the most pressing ethical issues in AI. AI systems often require vast amounts of data to function effectively. This reliance raises serious concerns about how personal information is collected, stored, and used. Imagine an AI healthcare system that analyzes patient records to predict diseases. While beneficial, the sensitive nature of this data demands stringent privacy measures. Unauthorized access or data breaches could jeopardize individuals' privacy and trust.

Bias and fairness in AI algorithms present another significant ethical challenge. AI systems learn from existing data, which can contain biases that get perpetuated in the AI's decisions. For instance, if an AI hiring tool is trained on biased data favoring certain demographics, it may unfairly discriminate against other groups. This issue underscores the importance of using diverse and representative datasets and implementing fairness checks to ensure equitable outcomes.

Accountability and transparency are also key concerns in AI ethics. When an AI system decides whether to approve a loan or diagnose a medical condition, it's crucial to understand how that decision was made. This transparency helps build trust and ensures that decisions can be audited and contested if necessary. For example, if an AI system denies a loan application, the applicant should have the right to know the reasons behind the decision and the ability to challenge it.

Another ethical dilemma concerns autonomy and control over AI systems. As AI becomes more autonomous, who is responsible for its actions? Consider autonomous vehicles that make split-second decisions to avoid accidents. If a self-driving car causes an accident, is the manufacturer, software developer, or AI to blame? Establishing clear guidelines for responsibility and control is essential to address these complex scenarios.

Philosophical debates on AI delve into deeper questions about the nature of machine consciousness and sentience. Can AI ever achieve a level of consciousness similar to humans? If so, what moral and ethical considerations arise? These questions challenge our understanding of consciousness and the ethical treatment of potentially sentient beings. The ethical considerations of AI-human interactions also come into play. As AI systems become more sophisticated, they may be used in roles that require empathy and understanding, such as caregiving or therapy. Ensuring that these interactions are ethical and beneficial is crucial.

The potential for AI to surpass human intelligence, known as superintelligence, raises existential questions. If AI reaches a level of intelligence far beyond human capabilities, what will be its impact on society? Will it enhance human life, or could it pose a threat to our very existence? These questions highlight the need for careful consideration and preparation for a future where superintelligent AI may become a reality.

Another area of philosophical inquiry is the moral status and rights of AI entities. If an AI system achieves a level of consciousness or sentience, should it be granted moral considerations or rights? This question challenges our current ethical frameworks and requires us to rethink our approach to non-human entities.

Looking to the future, the study of AI ethics and philosophy is evolving to address emerging trends and challenges. Developing comprehensive ethical frameworks for AI governance is a priority. These frameworks aim to ensure that AI technologies are developed and used responsibly, balancing innovation with ethical considerations. Promoting interdisciplinary collaboration between AI researchers and ethicists is also essential. These experts can develop robust ethical guidelines and address complex ethical dilemmas by working together.

Exploring AI's societal impact on global inequality and justice is another critical area of focus. AI has the potential to exacerbate existing inequalities or help bridge gaps. Ensuring that AI technologies are accessible and beneficial to all segments of society is a key ethical consideration. Finally, anticipating and addressing long-term existential risks associated with AI is crucial. As AI advances, it's essential to consider and prepare for potential risks that could have far-reaching consequences for humanity.

In summary, the ethical and philosophical discussions surrounding AI are vital to ensuring that these technologies benefit society while minimizing harm. We can navigate the complex landscape of AI ethics and philosophy by addressing key ethical issues, engaging in philosophical debates, and exploring future directions. This ongoing dialogue helps us understand and shape the role of AI in our lives, ensuring that its development aligns with our values and principles.

Next, we'll explore how AI is transforming education and the steps you can take to stay ahead in this rapidly evolving field.

Interactive Quiz: Special Topics in AI

1. Natural Language Processing (NLP): AI's Understanding of Human Language

Question: What is tokenization in NLP?

a) Breaking down text into smaller units like words or phrases.
b) Identifying the grammatical categories of words.
c) Detecting and classifying named entities.

Question: Which of the following is a real-world application of NLP?

a) Predicting stock market trends.
b) Translating languages in real time.
c) Creating virtual reality simulations.

2. Generative AI: Creating New Content with AI

Question: What is the purpose of Generative Adversarial Networks (GANs) in AI?

a) Detecting and classifying images.
b) Generating realistic data points by using two neural networks.
c) Analyzing large datasets for trends.

Question: Which of the following is an application of generative AI?

a) Autonomous vehicle navigation.
b) Generating realistic deepfake videos.
c) Performing sentiment analysis on social media posts.

3. AI in Ethics and Philosophy: Debating AI's Role in Society

Question: What is one key ethical concern related to AI?

- a) Lack of processing power.
- b) Bias and fairness in AI algorithms.
- c) Inability to automate tasks.

Question: Why is transparency important in AI decision-making?

a) It speeds up the AI's processing.

b) It allows users to understand and challenge AI decisions.

c) It ensures AI systems don't need updates.

WE'D LOVE YOUR FEEDBACK!

Thank you for joining us on this incredible journey into the world of AI! Your learning experience doesn't end here – it's just the beginning. But before you dive deeper, we'd really appreciate it if you could share your thoughts and insights with others.

Why Your Review Matters

"Sharing knowledge is the way we light up the path for others to follow."

Your feedback can help guide future readers who, like you, are eager to learn but may be unsure where to start. By leaving a review, you're not just sharing your experience, you're empowering others to embark on their AI journey with confidence and clarity.

How Was Your Journey?

Did the hands-on projects spark new ideas? Were the quizzes helpful in solidifying your understanding? Maybe you discovered a tool or concept that really clicked for you! Whether it's the big breakthroughs or the small wins, we'd love to hear about it all.

How to Leave a Review

Sharing your thoughts is easy and only takes a moment:

Simply click on the QR code and it will take you right to the review page.

Spread the Inspiration!

Your words can inspire others to take that first step toward understanding AI. Imagine the difference your review could make in helping someone else gain the skills and confidence to succeed.Thank you for being part of this learning adventure! Your voice matters, and we can't wait to read what you have to say.

CONCLUSION

We embarked on this journey with "Unlocking AI for Beginners" aiming to make AI accessible and engaging for everyone, regardless of their background. Our goal was to demystify AI, breaking down complex concepts into relatable terms and practical applications.

We began by laying the Foundations of AI, exploring its basics, history, and everyday applications. You learned how AI has evolved from a sci-fi concept to a transformative technology integrated into daily life. We then delved into Core Concepts and Mechanisms, where we unpacked machine learning, neural networks, and the crucial role of data in powering AI systems.

Next, we introduced you to various Tools and Technologies that make AI user-friendly. From no-code platforms to cloud-based services, you discovered how to build and deploy AI models without extensive coding knowledge. We moved on to Practical Applications, showcasing real-world examples across industries like healthcare, finance, retail, and transportation. These examples highlighted AI's potential to revolutionize various sectors.

We didn't stop at theory. Through Hands-On Projects, you engaged with interactive exercises that reinforced your understanding. Building your first AI model, creating a chatbot, and conducting sentiment analysis were not just tasks but steps towards mastering AI.

Understanding the Ethical and Societal Implications of AI is crucial. We discussed privacy, bias, accountability, and the societal impact of AI technologies. These considerations ensure that AI development aligns with ethical standards and benefits everyone fairly.

Looking ahead, we explored Future Trends in AI, such as quantum computing, AI in space exploration, and emerging technologies like explainable AI and neuromorphic computing. These trends offer a glimpse into the exciting possibilities that lie ahead.

We also provided guidance on Career Prospects in AI, helping you leverage your newfound knowledge for career growth. We covered the steps to advance your career, from identifying in-demand skills to transitioning into AI roles and obtaining certifications.

To ensure you stay updated, we offered Resources for Continuous Learning. Online courses, books, conferences, podcasts, and curated resource lists are invaluable tools for ongoing education. Staying curious and continuously learning is key to thriving in the ever-evolving AI landscape.

We took a closer look at Special Topics in AI, such as Natural Language Processing (NLP), generative AI, and AI ethics. These deep dives provided a comprehensive understanding of specific AI areas, enhancing your overall knowledge.

By now, you should have a solid understanding of AI fundamentals and core concepts. The practical skills gained through hands-on projects and interactive exercises are invaluable. Ethical awareness is crucial in guiding responsible AI development and usage. You are now equipped to stay updated with AI advancements and trends, ready to apply your knowledge in various contexts.

The book discusses career advancement strategies that will help you transition into AI roles and grow in your current career. But this journey doesn't end here. I encourage you to apply what you've learned by engaging in personal projects, exploring new AI tools, and participating in the AI community. Stay curious, keep learning, and leverage the resources and strategies provided in the book.

Thank you for joining me on this exciting journey into the world of AI. Your time and engagement are greatly appreciated. I invite you to share your thoughts, experiences, and any questions you may have. Your feedback is invaluable and helps improve future editions.

Remember, AI is accessible to everyone. You now have the tools and knowledge to explore and excel in this fascinating field. Embrace the opportunities, stay confident, and continue to unlock the potential of AI. The future is bright, and your journey has just begun.

QUIZ ANSWERS

Chapter 1 Answers
1.a, a
2.b, b
3.c, b
4.b, b
5.b, a
Chapter 2 Answers
1.b, b
2.b, b
3.a, b
4.c, b
5.b, b
Chapter 3 Answers
1.a, b
2.b, c
3.a, a
4.b, b
5.b, b
Chapter 4 Answers
1.b, b
2.b, b
3.b, b
4.b, b
5.b, b
Chapter 5 Answers
1.b, c
2.b, c
3.b, a
4.b, b
5.b, b
Chapter 6 Answers
1.a, b
2.b, b
3.b, b

4.b, b
5.a, a

Chapter 7 Answers
1.b, b
2.a, b
3.b, b
4.b, b
5.b, b

Chapter 8 Answers
1.b, b
2.b, b
3.b, b
4.b, b
5.a, b

Chapter 9 Answers
1.c, b
2.b, b
3.a, b
4.b, b
5.b, b

Chapter 10 Answers
1.a, b
2.b, b
3.b, b

REFERENCES

- *The History of Artificial Intelligence: Complete AI Timeline* https://www.techtarget.com/searchenterpriseai/tip/The-history-of-artificial-intelligence-Complete-AI-timeline
- *The Turing Test (Stanford Encyclopedia of Philosophy)* https://plato.stanford.edu/entries/turing-test/
- *The three different types of Artificial Intelligence – ANI, AGI ...* https://www.ediweekly.com/the-three-different-types-of-artificial-intelligence-ani-agi-and-asi/
- *Deep Learning Breakthroughs: From AlphaGo to GPT-3* https://www.thebestblogever.co/blog/deep-learning-breakthroughs-from-alphago-to-gpt-3
- *What Is Machine Learning? Definition, Types, Applications ...* https://www.spiceworks.com/tech/artificial-intelligence/articles/what-is-ml/
- *Explained: Neural networks* https://news.mit.edu/2017/explained-neural-networks-deep-learning-0414
- *Introduction to Deep Learning* https://www.geeksforgeeks.org/introduction-deep-learning/
- *20 Examples of Generative AI Applications Across Industries* https://www.coursera.org/articles/generative-ai-applications
- *Revolutionizing healthcare: the role of artificial intelligence in ...* https://bmcmededuc.biomedcentral.com/articles/10.1186/s12909-023-04698-z
- *The Role of AI in Financial Services: From Robo-Advisors to ...* https://skillfloor.medium.com/the-role-of-ai-in-financial-services-from-robo-advisors-to-fraud-detection-810108aaf8af
- *How AI is Revolutionizing Retail Customer Service and ...* https://www.matrixflows.com/blog/retail-ai-customer-service
- *The Impact of Artificial Intelligence (AI) on Transportation ...* https://tcitransportation.com/blog/the-impact-of-artificial-intelligence-ai-on-transportation-logistics/#:~
- *The Complete No-Code AI Guide (Updated January 2024)* https://www.akkio.com/post/no-code-ai-tools-complete-guide
- *Step-by-step Guide On Building a Chatbot Using DialogFlow* https://marutitech.com/build-a-chatbot-using-dialogflow/

- *Beginner's Guide to Everything Image Recognition* https://medium.com/swlh/beginners-guide-to-everything-image-recognition-50771e786601
- *Top AI-powered Sentiment Analytics Tools for 2023* https://aithority.com/technology/analytics/from-text-to-emotions-top-ai-powered-sentiment-analytics-tools-for-2023/
- *The 7 Best AI Platforms: Your Guide to Making a Smart ...* https://www.pecan.ai/blog/best-ai-platforms-guide/
- *Google's Teachable Machine AI: Step-By-Step Tutorial Included* https://vinaykumarmoluguri.medium.com/googles-teachable-machine-ai-step-by-step-tutorial-included-6a7200199932
- *Getting started with Watson Assistant* https://cloud.ibm.com/docs/assistant?topic=assistant-getting-started
- *The Complete No-Code AI Guide (Updated January 2024)* https://www.akkio.com/post/no-code-ai-tools-complete-guide
- *The IEEE Global Initiative on Ethics of Autonomous and Intelligent Systems (A/IS)* https://www.researchgate.net/publication/332458783_The_IEEE_Global_Initiative_on_Ethics_of_Autonomous_and_Intelligent_Systems
- *Facial Recognition Technology vs Privacy: The Case of Clearview AI* https://qmro.qmul.ac.uk/xmlui/bitstream/handle/123456789/80559/1%20-%20Facial%20Recognition%20Technology%20%28Article%29.pdf?sequence=1&isAllowed=y
- *CCPA vs. GDPR: Similarities and Differences Explained* https://www.okta.com/blog/2021/04/ccpa-vs-gdpr/
- *AI Bias In Recruitment: Ethical Implications And ...* https://www.forbes.com/sites/forbestechcouncil/2023/09/25/ai-bias-in-recruitment-ethical-implications-and-transparency/
- *Want the Latest AI News? These 10 Websites Are a Must- ...* https://www.jeffbullas.com/ai-news/
- *Best AI Newsletters to Stay Informed about the Latest Trends* https://clickup.com/blog/best-ai-newsletters/
- *TOP-30 AI Influencers to Follow on Twitter by 2023* https://bytescout.com/blog/ai-influencers-to-follow-on-twitter.html
- *Top AI Conferences 2023: Roundup Of Top ...* https://www.forbes.com/sites/qai/2023/02/20/top-ai-conferences-2023-roundup-of-top-ai-conferences/
- *The Future of Jobs Report 2023 | World Economic Forum* https://www.weforum.org/publications/the-future-of-jobs-report-2023/digest/
- *Best AI Certifications | A Comprehensive Guide for 2024* https://medium.

com/@saiwadotai/best-ai-certifications-a-comprehensive-guide-for-2024-ae0924612eb5

- *How AI research and innovation is being used in non-tech ...* https://career.ufl.edu/how-ai-research-and-innovation-is-being-used-in-non-tech-careers/
- *How to Build A Stand-Out Artificial Intelligence Portfolio?* https://www.springboard.com/blog/data-science/ai-portfolio/
- *Reinforcement Learning: An Introduction* http://incompleteideas.net/book/the-book-2nd.html
- *Quantum Computers Can Run Powerful AI That Works like ...* https://www.scientificamerican.com/article/quantum-computers-can-run-powerful-ai-that-works-like-the-brain/
- *Here's How AI Is Changing NASA's Mars Rover Science* https://www.jpl.nasa.gov/news/heres-how-ai-is-changing-nasas-mars-rover-science
- *Top 8 Big Data Platforms and Tools in 2024* https://www.turing.com/resources/best-big-data-platforms
- *Top 20 Artificial Intelligence Books For Beginners 2024* https://www.mygreatlearning.com/blog/artificial-intelligence-books/
- *The 10 Best AI Courses That Are Worth Taking in 2024* https://www.techrepublic.com/article/best-ai-courses/
- *Four trends that changed AI in 2023* https://www.technologyreview.com/2023/12/19/1085696/four-trends-that-changed-ai-in-2023/
- *Ethical concerns mount as AI takes bigger decision-making ...* https://news.harvard.edu/gazette/story/2020/10/ethical-concerns-mount-as-ai-takes-bigger-decision-making-role/

ABOUT THE AUTHOR

Synergy AI Editions is a forward-thinking publishing company dedicated to making the world of AI accessible to everyone. With our first book, *Understanding Generative AI for Business Leaders*, and our second book, *Unlock AI for Beginners*, we focus on delivering clear, practical, and engaging resources tailored to meet the needs of both professionals and beginners alike.

We're passionate about your learning journey and committed to your success. Our mission is to simplify complex AI concepts so that you can confidently apply them in your personal or professional life. Every book we produce is designed with your growth in mind, combining hands-on exercises, real-world examples, and interactive learning experiences.

As we continue to expand our catalog, we value your feedback and insights. Your experience shapes how we craft future resources, ensuring our books remain relevant, practical, and supportive of your goals. Together, we can navigate the evolving landscape of AI and unlock new opportunities for learning and success.

Thank you for being a part of our community—we're excited to keep growing with you!